fun with
one block quilts

12 Projects in Multiple Sizes from 1 Simple Block

CHERYL MALKOWSKI

C&T PUBLISHING

Text © 2007 Cheryl Malkowski

Artwork © 2007 C&T Publishing, Inc.

PUBLISHER: Amy Marson

EDITORIAL DIRECTOR: Gailen Runge

ACQUISITIONS EDITOR: Jan Grigsby

EDITORS: Kesel Wilson & Jack Braunstein

TECHNICAL EDITORS: Susan Nelsen & Rene Steinpress

PROOFREADER/COPYEDITOR: Wordfirm Inc.

COVER DESIGNER/BOOK DESIGNER: Kristen Yenche

ILLUSTRATOR: Kirstie L. Pettersen

PRODUCTION COORDINATORS: Kiera Lofgreen & Kerry Graham

Photography by C&T Publishing, Inc., unless otherwise noted

Published by C&T Publishing, Inc., P.O. Box 1456, Lafayette, CA 94549

Library of Congress Cataloging-in-Publication Data
Malkowski, Cheryl.

Fun with one block quilts : 12 projects in multiple sizes from 1 simple block / Cheryl Malkowski.

    p. cm.

    ISBN-13: 978-1-57120-391-5 (paper trade : alk. paper)

    ISBN-10: 1-57120-391-5 (paper trade : alk. paper)

    1. Patchwork--Patterns. 2. Quilting--Patterns. I. Title.

    TT835.M27176 2007

    746.46'041—dc22

            2006030715

Printed in China

10 9 8 7 6 5 4 3 2 1

Dedication

For Mom and Dad. Thanks for believing in me.

Acknowledgments

Many thanks to the ladies of the Umpqua Quilters Guild and the Tuesday Night Quilters Frenzy group at Country Lady Quilt Shop in Roseburg, Oregon, who agreed to try out these patterns and make quilts for the gallery. Without their help and the help of the amazingly supportive staff at Country Lady, I'd have spent many more long months in front of the sewing machine. Their technical input and creative twists on my simple idea have been inspiring and invaluable!

Special thanks to Jane Yurk, who took on extra work when I needed time to write, and to Charlie Weckerle, who is always offering encouragement and help, not to mention the use of her longarm quilting machine. Thanks!

Superior Threads sent me some beautiful King Tut extra-long-staple cotton thread to quilt some of my samples with. It is a joy to work with almost completely lint-free thread, and it is so beautiful as well! Thank you so much. Now I'm hooked!

Many thanks to Prym Consumer USA, whose lines include the Omnigrid, Omnigrip, and Collins products used in this book. These products simplify quilting and make accuracy possible for even novice quilters.

The staff of C&T Publishing are wonderful to work with in every respect. I love how well they listen, catch the vision, and run with an idea. It feels great when they turn my doodles into something real.

My husband, Tom, has been very patient with me, especially when all I want to do is write and he's full of ideas for doing something fun (can we go see that movie now?). I would have liked to thank Bosco, my dog, for allowing me the time to do this project, but he didn't willingly give me my space to work. When I wouldn't play with him, he pouted in the utility room. He did seem to listen, though (or at least hang around when I was talking myself through materials lists and cutting instructions), and that was a comfort.

Contents

Projects

Play Time, 55″ × 38¹/₂″, 2005 Cheryl Malkowski.

Introduction

Can I tell you a story about how I made the *Play Time* quilt shown above? Once, just for fun, I made a beautiful quilt from Jan Krentz's book *Hunter Star Quilts and Beyond*. Of course, I didn't want to do it exactly like hers so I made a bunch of half-square triangle blocks to put around the outside for a border. Only, I failed to measure the quilt center to make sure they would fit where they needed to go. Let's just say that the quilt now has plain borders and I was left with a stack of these blocks in all of my favorite colors of dark batiks. So, I dug through my fabric stash to make squares of light fabrics. I put the light squares on top of the dark half-square triangle blocks, cut them diagonally, and stitched them along the bias. The result was two blocks with three triangles each (two quarter-squares and one half-square), but the blocks were *mirror images*.

I used those first Y Blocks to make the *Play Time* quilt and found as I played with them that they could be used to form lots of interesting patterns and designs. That made sense since these units have long been used in many traditional patchwork quilts. They can be used to make stars and pinwheels, diagonal lines, and much more. They were generally just fun to play with and a great starting point for a burst of creativity. I found I could design quilts that ranged from very traditional to very artsy just using the Y Block with a few half-squares and plain blocks thrown in once in a while. This was really exciting, but I soon noticed that they didn't get along with their neighbors very well. That one long diagonal seam was not nesting with the seams in the next block all the time, and the result was lumpy, unmatched seams. *This book addresses that issue and supplies some great tips for perfectly matched, no-fear triangles every time!*

Making Y Blocks

Y Block

The Y Block is a component of numerous classic blocks such as the Double Windmill, Whirlwind, and Martha Washington Star. These blocks have been around for a long time so there are many methods for making the Y Block. Since it uses both half- and quarter-square triangles, you will often see methods for construction that include drawing a diagonal line and stitching on both sides of that line. While the quilt police will not come after you if you use this technique, I should warn you: *the standard line-drawing technique does not yield the results you need for the patterns in this book.* That technique gives you two mirror-image blocks, and what you need are identical blocks.

My method for making Y Blocks was born out of this need for identical blocks. As they say, necessity is the mother of all invention! My process is all about 1, 2, 3. When you orient a block so that the half-square triangle is in the lower right corner, the seams naturally form a lowercase Y. Each triangle is assigned a number, and if you can get the 1, 2, 3 in your head and sew a ¼˝ seam allowance, you'll be chain stitching beautiful Y Blocks in no time!

TOOLS

All you need to make Y Blocks are regular quilting tools with a few extras. Those extras include some see-through colored tape (such as Omnigrid Glow-Line Tape) and a 6½˝ square ruler with a smooth underside and a diagonal line that runs from corner to corner. Use the tape to mark the underside of the ruler. This gives you a place to nest the ruler for a firm grip while cutting.

Another handy tool is a ¼˝ presser foot or other guide. There is no substitute for a good ¼˝ seam allowance. *Do whatever you have to do to achieve it.* Some machines come equipped with fences or bars that sit in front of the presser foot. If yours doesn't, try measuring from your needle and marking your ¼˝ with a Collins Machine Seam Gauge and Adhesive Guide, or use several layers of painter's tape or an ⅛˝-high stack of sticky notes.

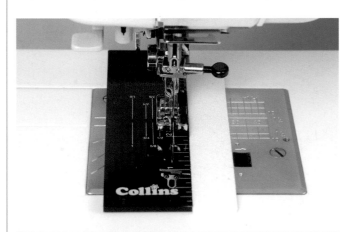

An accurate ¼˝ seam allowance is absolutely critical.

> **Tip**
> You will find that you get fewer instances of fabric munching by your machine if you use a single-stitch needle plate. This plate has only a tiny round hole where the needle goes up and down instead of the wider hole used for zigzag stitches, so there is simply no room for the fabric to get caught.

FABRIC PREPARATION

If you are concerned about stitching on the cut bias edge, let me give you a few suggestions to help stabilize your fabric. Begin by prewashing the fabric (if you don't want to prewash, be prepared to use a dye magnet product such as Retayne when you launder your quilt). After washing, press the fabric with spray starch to give it stiffness before you cut it. There is nothing scary about sewing together these paperlike pieces. Just handle them gently and let your machine pull the fabric while you stitch.

KEEPING TRACK OF FABRIC POSITIONS

The patterns in this book call for specific placement of fabric to achieve the designs. The most essential thing to remember about Y Blocks is the fabric positioning. If the fabrics are not in the right positions when you are cutting and stitching the Position 1 and Position 2 triangles, the result is a mirror image of the block you are trying to make. That will never do, so here is a way to make sure your blocks look like what you had in mind: When you need to figure out where a fabric goes in a block, orient the block so it looks like a lowercase letter Y. Position 1 is the quarter-square triangle on the lower left side. Position 2 is the quarter-square triangle on top, and Position 3 is the half-square triangle on the lower right side.

Use this diagram as a guide for creating your Y Blocks.

In the Block Construction charts in the projects, you will see blank block diagrams that you can use when planning your projects. Draw a matching sketch large enough that you can glue small scraps of fabric in their proper positions. This will help you remember the right fabric position when it is time to cut or sew. Be sure to label your sketch so you know which end is the top.

POSITIONS 1 & 2: THE ¼-SQUARE TRIANGLES

1. Let's start by making the Y Block pictured on page 5. Cut a square each of Position 1 and Position 2 fabric that is 1½″ larger than the *finished* block. For example, if you are making 5″ square finished blocks, cut these fabrics 6½″ × 6½″. For every pair of Position 1 and Position 2 squares you cut, you have enough quarter-square triangles to make 4 completed Y Blocks when the Position 3 fabric is added.

2. Place the Position 1 and Position 2 fabrics right sides together on the cutting mat. The Position 2 fabric goes on the bottom and the Position 1 fabric on top. If you have done this correctly you will be looking at the wrong side of the Position 1 fabric when you go to make your cut. Cut this stack twice diagonally from corner to corner.

Position 1 fabric is always on top when you are making the crosscut.

3. Keeping the Position 1 fabric on top, stack the pairs of triangles so that the right angle (the 90° angle) points to the upper right. This square edge is easier to feed under the presser foot. Stacking the triangles this way by your sewing machine means everything is positioned correctly to start your chain stitching.

Position the triangle pairs just like this.

Tip If you stack the pairs of triangles unevenly, they'll be easier to pick up when you are ready to sew the pairs together.

4. Chain stitch the triangles together along the right edge using a ¼˝ seam allowance.

Chain stitching

5. Take the chain-stitched quarter-square triangles to your pressing surface like a string of flags and press *toward* the Position 2 fabric.

Pressing the chain-stitched work

To ensure really precise points, you need a good iron and good pressing habits. Place the chain-stitched pieces on the ironing board with the seam allowance away from you. Set the seam by pressing the newly sewn pieces while they are still right sides together. Lift the top fabric

and glide the tip of the iron along the seam to be pressed open, making sure you get in right to the thread along the whole seam and nudge it over. Press the rest of the block with an up and down motion for the least distortion.

6. Clip the threads between the units to separate them.

ADDING THE POSITION 3 TRIANGLE

1. Cut 2 squares of the Position 3 fabric 1˝ larger than the *finished* square. For example, for 5˝ square finished blocks, cut this fabric 6˝ × 6˝. Cut the squares once diagonally from corner to corner. Two squares of the Position 3 fabric will complete 4 Y Blocks when added to the Position 1 and Position 2 units.

Tip Don't trim these yet! This Position 1 and 2 unit is intentionally larger than the Position 3 triangle so you can align the long bias edge and still be able to line up the opposing point of the Position 3 triangle with the seam allowance of the pieced triangle.

2. Place these half-squares right sides together on *top* of the half-squares you made from the Position 1 and Position 2 fabrics. Make sure the diagonal edges are even and match the right-angle point of the Position 3 fabric with the seamline of the pieced half-square.

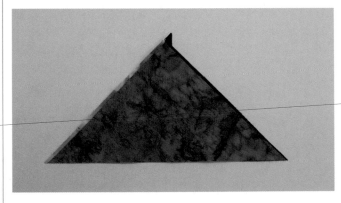

Align the Position 3 half-squares with the Position 1 and 2 half-squares, right sides together.

3. Chain stitch the blocks together along the diagonal edge.

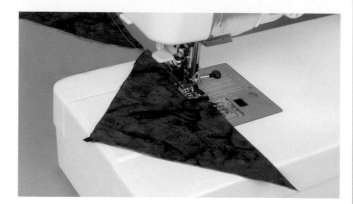

Chain stitch units together.

Squaring Up

Before pressing the block open, you need to square the block to 5½" × 5½". You can use any square ruler with a flat underside for this. To help hold it in exactly the right place for cutting, I like to use Omnigrid Glow-Line Tape to mark the seamlines. It is a translucent colored tape that is easy to see and easy to remove.

1. Place your square ruler on a flat surface with the underside facing up. Put some tape just to the left side of the printed diagonal line, so when you align the seam between the 2 small triangles you can see that the line is directly on top of the stitching.

2. Place another piece of tape along the line corresponding to the size of the *unfinished* block—5½" for our example block. This line should be perpendicular to the diagonal line and form the outlines of Position 1 and Position 2 on the ruler. Make sure the tape is just inside the marked line, not on top of it. *This ruler should now give you perfect squares every time.*

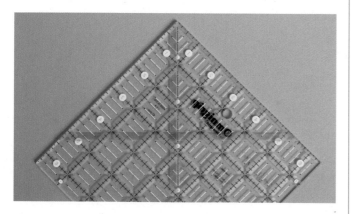

Marking the ruler

3. Take the chain of triangles to the cutting mat with the pieced side facing up and the long seam allowance closest to you. Before the square is pressed at the seam allowance, square it to the unfinished size. Check the first few blocks as they are cut to see if your tape is placed correctly. The diagonal seams should come right to the corners of the squares. Adjust if necessary.

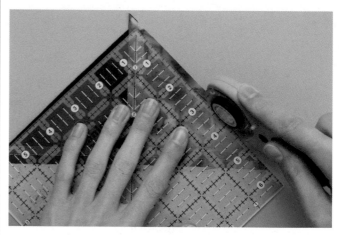

Squaring up

> **Tip**
> Position your hand holding the ruler so that there is pressure all around the outer edges, especially the top point, so that nothing moves while you're cutting.

4. Press *toward* the large Position 3 triangle and trim the dog-ears.

Stacking blocks

Now consider them as 3 separate seam allowances. You'll see that 2 of them go counterclockwise. Press the last one (the right side of the long seam allowance) so that it goes counterclockwise as well. This enables you to fit any Y Block into any position in your quilt without interference from neighboring seam allowances.

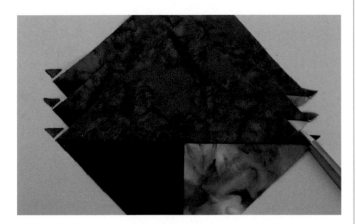

Trimming dog-ears

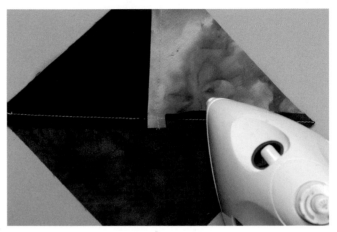

Pressing all seams counterclockwise

CLIP & FLIP PRESSING

For some patterns, where the blocks play well together or where they don't actually touch or meet at the corners, your block is complete. In other cases, where the block is rotated in different ways, there is one more step: Clip & Flip Pressing. *The project patterns note whether this step is required.* **Look for the Clip & Flip icon next to the project name.**

Once the blocks are complete, the last step is to turn them wrong side up so that the long seam is running horizontally. Clip the long seam allowance almost to the stitching, just to the right of the center seam.

Clipping the long seam

Finishing Your Quilt

After you've made your quilt top, you're going to want to finish it up! For some people, this is the hardest part, but it is worth it. Putting the finishing touches on your creation will give you enormous satisfaction.

BATTING

Choose your batting based on how the quilt will be quilted and used. A natural-fiber batting is easier to handle in a domestic machine because it generally clings to the fabric better than polyester. If you are sending your quilt out to a longarm quilter, the fiber won't matter as much, but your quilter could have preferences, so ask him or her. Polyester may give you an initially higher loft but will flatten with time and won't shrink. Cotton and poly/cotton blends usually look flatter initially but often pucker with time. Be sure to read the label on the batting package to determine whether it will meet your needs.

QUILTING

Most of the quilts in this book don't have a lot of empty space built in for elaborate quilting. My suggestion is to use an interesting all-over design. There are many wonderful books available with ideas for quilting motifs and patterns. Another option is to take your quilt to a local quilting professional. Your quilt shop should be able to provide you with names of local experts.

BINDING

Once the quilting is done, you can bind your quilt. The fabric requirements in this book allow for a double-fold binding. When you have a pieced outer border, like many of these quilts have, you will need a rather narrow binding so you don't hide the triangle points. I use a 2″-wide binding strip and leave a smidgen of extra batting and backing around the outside of the quilt top.

1. Cut the required number of strips to go around your quilt.

2. Stitch the strips together end-to-end with diagonal seams and press the strips in half lengthwise with wrong sides together.

3. Pick a beginning point on the quilt edge to add the binding, not at a corner and not in the center. Starting about 8″ from the end of the binding strip and using a walking foot, begin stitching a ¼″ seam. Stop stitching ¼″ from the corner, backstitch, and remove the quilt from under the needle.

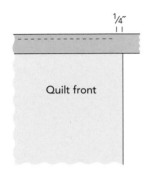

Stop stitching ¼″ from corner. Backstitch.

4. Fold the binding straight up, forming a 45° angle. Then bring the binding straight down, aligning the edge of the binding with the quilt edge and the newly formed fold of the binding even with the top edge of the quilt. Begin stitching at the top edge, using a ¼″ seam again. Continue stitching the sides and corners to about 10″ from the beginning binding strip, and stop.

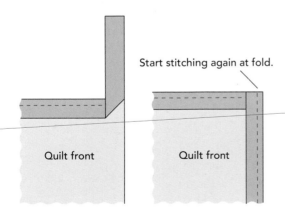

Fold binding up, then fold it down. Begin sewing.

5. Open up and cut a clean square edge on the beginning binding strip. Measure the width of your binding strip and mark a pencil mark that distance from the newly cut end. Cut the ending binding strip so it overlaps to the pencil mark on the beginning strip when the strips are lined up as shown.

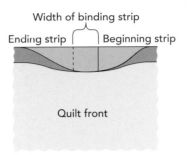

Overlapping ends

6. Referring to the diagram, arrange the strip ends right sides together at a right angle. Mark a diagonal line from corner to corner. Stitch on the line and check to make sure that the binding fits. Then trim the seam allowance to ¼″. Press the seam allowance to one side.

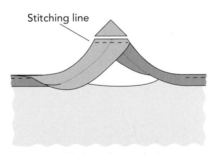

Stitch on line and trim.

Check fit before trimming seam.

7. Stitch the remainder of the binding to the quilt and hand stitch the binding to the back of the quilt.

 Remember to label your work. Someone will want to know who was responsible for bringing this bit of beauty into the world!

Whirlwind 66″ × 90″

2005 Cheryl Malkowski
Pieced by Karol Orth. Quilted by Ramonda Weckerle.

Whirlwind

This fun quilt is a great starter project. It's a good introduction to using the Y Block to create beautiful designs.

For this quilt, I've included instructions for making 3 different sizes. You can make the 54″ × 66″ or 66″ × 90″ quilt, or go for the giant 90″ × 102″ quilt, whichever suits your fancy.

FABRIC REQUIREMENTS Yardage is based on 42″-wide fabric unless noted.

Fabric	54″ × 66″ Quilt	66″ × 90″ Quilt	90″ × 102″ Quilt
Blue	1⅜ yds	2 yds	3 yds
Green	1⅛ yds	1¾ yds	2¾ yds
Fuchsia print	2½ yds	3¾ yds	5⅝ yds
Blue (for binding)	½ yd	⅝ yd	¾ yd
Batting	58″ × 70″	70″ × 94″	94″ × 106″
108″-wide backing	1⅔ yds	2 yds	2¾ yds

CUTTING BLOCKS Strips are cut across width of fabric, selvage to selvage.

Fabric	54″ × 66″ Quilt	66″ × 90″ Quilt	90″ × 102″ Quilt
Blue	• From 3 strips 7½″ wide, cut: 12 squares 7½″ × 7½″	• From 5 strips 7½″ wide, cut: 24 squares 7½″ × 7½″	• From 9 strips 7½″ wide, cut: 42 squares 7½″ × 7½″
Green	• From 4 strips 7½″ wide, cut: 20 squares 7½″ × 7½″	• From 7 strips 7½″ wide, cut: 35 squares 7½″ × 7½″	• From 12 strips 7½″ wide, cut: 56 squares 7½″ × 7½″
Fuchsia print	• From 2 strips 7½″ wide, cut: 8 squares 7½″ × 7½″ • From 8 strips 7″ wide, cut: 40 squares 7″ × 7″ • From 1 strip 6½″ wide, cut: 4 squares 6½″ × 6½″	• From 3 strips 7½″ wide, cut: 11 squares 7½″ × 7½″ 4 squares 6½″ × 6½″ • From 14 strips 7″ wide, cut: 70 squares 7″ × 7″	• From 3 strips 7½″ wide, cut: 14 squares 7½″ × 7½″ • From 23 strips 7″ wide, cut: 112 squares 7″ × 7″ • From 1 strip 6½″ wide, cut: 4 squares 6½″ × 6½″

BLOCK CONSTRUCTION

Sketch numbered blocks and glue small pieces of fabric to them to remind you of your color placement. Follow the directions for making Y Blocks on pages 5–9.

	54″ × 66″ Quilt	66″ × 90″ Quilt	90″ × 102″ Quilt
Finished block size	6″ × 6″	6″ × 6″	6″ × 6″
Position 1 & 2 square size	7½″ × 7½″	7½″ × 7½″	7½″ × 7½″
Position 3 square size	7″ × 7″	7″ × 7″	7″ × 7″
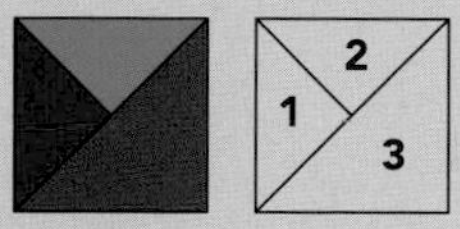 Block A	Make 48 from: 12 Position 1 & 2 24 Position 3	Make 96 from: 24 Position 1 & 2 48 Position 3	Make 168 from: 42 Position 1 & 2 84 Position 3
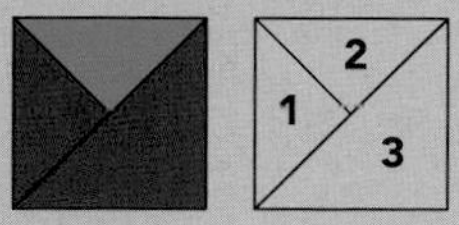 Block B	Make 32 from: 8 Position 1 & 2 16 Position 3	Make 44 from: 11 Position 1 & 2 22 Position 3	Make 56 from: 14 Position 1 & 2 28 Position 3
Whirlwind blocks	Make 12 from: 48 A Blocks	Make 24 from: 96 A Blocks	Make 42 from: 168 A Blocks

QUILT ASSEMBLY			
	54″ × 66″ Quilt	**66″ × 90″ Quilt**	**90″ × 102″ Quilt**
Quilt center layout	4 rows of 3 Whirlwind blocks ($36\frac{1}{2}″ \times 48\frac{1}{2}″$)	6 rows of 4 Whirlwind blocks ($48\frac{1}{2}″ \times 72\frac{1}{2}″$)	7 rows of 6 Whirlwind blocks ($72\frac{1}{2}″ \times 84\frac{1}{2}″$)

BORDERS AND BINDING Strips are cut across width of fabric, selvage to selvage.			
Fabric	**54″ × 66″ Quilt**	**66″ × 90″ Quilt**	**90″ × 102″ Quilt**
Blue	• Join 5 strips $3\frac{1}{2}″$ wide; cut: 2 pieces $36\frac{1}{2}″$ long 2 pieces $54\frac{1}{2}″$ long	• Join 7 strips $3\frac{1}{2}″$ wide; cut: 2 pieces $48\frac{1}{2}″$ long 2 pieces $78\frac{1}{2}″$ long	• Join 9 strips $3\frac{1}{2}″$ wide; cut: 2 pieces $72\frac{1}{2}″$ long 2 pieces $90\frac{1}{2}″$ long
Binding	• Cut 7 strips 2″ wide	• Cut 8 strips 2″ wide	• Cut 10 strips 2″ wide

BLOCK BORDERS			
	54″ × 66″ Quilt	**66″ × 90″ Quilt**	**90″ × 102″ Quilt**
Blocks per row	• Top and bottom, each: 7 B Blocks	• Top and bottom, each: 9 B Blocks	• Top and bottom, each: 13 B Blocks
	• Each side: 9 B Blocks plus 2 fuchsia $6\frac{1}{2}″ \times 6\frac{1}{2}″$ squares	• Each side: 13 B Blocks plus 2 fuchsia $6\frac{1}{2}″ \times 6\frac{1}{2}″$ squares	• Each side: 15 B Blocks plus 2 fuchsia $6\frac{1}{2}″ \times 6\frac{1}{2}″$ squares

Quilt Assembly

1. Arrange and stitch together the A Blocks in groups of 4 to make Whirlwind blocks. Press toward the Position 3 fabric, clipping where necessary.

Whirlwind block

2. Use the Quilt Assembly chart, diagram, and project photo to arrange the Whirlwind blocks into rows. Sew the rows and press the seam allowances to one side. Sew the rows together to form the quilt center.

Borders

1. Use the Borders and Binding chart to prepare the $3\frac{1}{2}″$-wide blue inner border strips.

2. Stitch the 2 short inner border pieces to the top and bottom of the quilt. Then add the 2 long pieces to the sides of the quilt. Press toward the border.

3. Use the Block Borders chart to determine the number of blocks to stitch for 2 rows of B Block borders for the top and bottom of the quilt. Press toward the inside.

4. Again referring to the Block Borders chart, stitch 2 rows of B Block borders for the sides of the quilt. Add a fuchsia $6\frac{1}{2}″ \times 6\frac{1}{2}″$ square to each end. Press toward the inside.

5. Attach the B Block borders to the sides of the quilt and press toward the inside.

Quilt assembly diagram, 66″ × 90″

Twisty Star
Table Runner

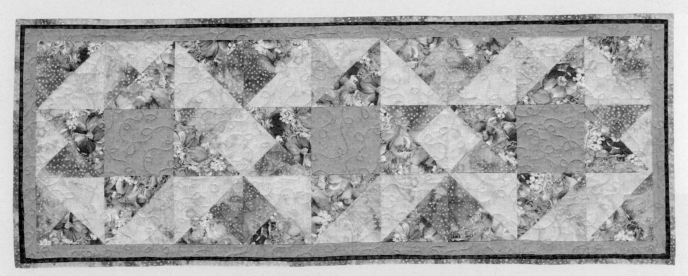

Twisty Star Table Runner, 38″ × 14″, 2005 Cheryl Malkowski.

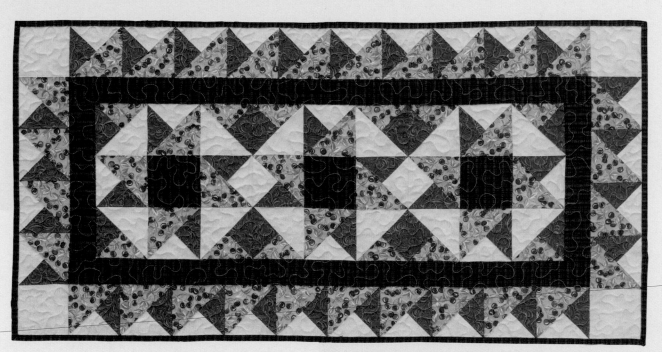

Twisty Star Bordered Table Runner, 36″ × 18″, 2005 Cheryl Malkowski.

Brighten your table or dresser top with these fun, easy runners or give them as gifts and become somebody's favorite quilter.

For this project, you have 2 size options. The 38″ × 14″ runner uses 4″ blocks and the 36″ × 18″ runner uses 3″ blocks.

FABRIC REQUIREMENTS Yardage is based on 42″-wide fabric unless noted.		
Fabric	**38″ × 14″ Quilt**	**36″ × 18″ Quilt**
Multi-print	½ yd	½ yd
Orange dot (includes binding)	½ yd	*Not applicable*
Light green	½ yd	½ yd
Lavender	⅜ yd	*Not applicable*
Red check (includes binding)	*Not applicable*	⅝ yd
Red	⅛ yd	½ yd
Backing	½ yd	⅝ yd
Batting	42″ × 18″	40″ × 22″

CUTTING BLOCKS Strips are cut across width of fabric, selvage to selvage.		
Fabric	**38″ × 14″ Quilt**	**36″ × 18″ Quilt**
Multi-print	• From 1 strip 5½″ wide, cut: 4 squares 5½″ × 5½″ • From 1 strip 5″ wide, cut: 6 squares 5″ × 5″	• From 1 strip 4½″ wide, cut: 4 squares 4½″ × 4½″ • From 2 strips 4″ wide, cut: 20 squares 4″ × 4″
Orange dot	• From 1 strip 5½″ wide, cut: 7 squares 5½″ × 5½″	*Not applicable*
Light green	• From 1 strip 5½″ wide, cut: 3 squares 5½″ × 5½″ • From 1 strip 5″ wide, cut: 6 squares 5″ × 5″	• From 2 strips 4½″ wide, cut: 10 squares 4½″ × 4½″ • From 1 strip 4″ wide, cut: 6 squares 4″ × 4″ 4 squares 3½″ × 3½″
Lavender	• From 1 strip 4½″ wide, cut: 3 squares 4½″ × 4½″	*Not applicable*
Red check	*Not applicable*	• From 1 strip 3½″ wide, cut: 3 squares 3½″ × 3½″
Red	*Not applicable*	• From 2 strips 4½″ wide, cut: 14 squares 4½″ × 4½″

BLOCK CONSTRUCTION Use Clip & Flip Pressing.

Sketch numbered blocks and glue small pieces of fabric to them to remind you of your color placement. Follow the directions for making Y Blocks on pages 5–9.

	38″ × 14″ Quilt
Finished block size	4″ × 4″
Position 1 & 2 square size	5½″ × 5½″
Position 3 square size	5″ × 5″
Block A	Make 12 from: 3 Position 1 & 2, 6 Position 3
Block B	Make 6 from: 2 Position 1 & 2, 3 Position 3 (yields 2 extra 1 & 2 units)
Block C	Make 6 from: 2 Position 1 & 2, 3 Position 3 (yields 2 extra 1 & 2 units)
	36″ × 18″ Quilt
Finished block size	3″ × 3″
Position 1 & 2 square size	4½″ × 4½″
Position 3 square size	4″ × 4″
Block A	Make 40 from: 10 Position 1 & 2, 20 Position 3
Block B	Make 6 from: 2 Position 1 & 2, 3 Position 3 (yields 2 extra 1 & 2 units)
Block C	Make 6 from: 2 Position 1 & 2, 3 Position 3 (yields 2 extra 1 & 2 units)

QUILT ASSEMBLY									
Row 1	B	A	C	B	A	C	B	A	C
Row 2	A		A	A		A	A		A
Row 3	C	A	B	C	A	B	C	A	B

BORDERS AND BINDING Strips are cut across width of fabric, selvage to selvage.		
Fabric	**38″ × 14″ Quilt**	**36″ × 18″ Quilt**
Lavender	• From 3 strips 1¼″ wide, cut: 2 pieces 12½″ long 2 pieces 38″ long	*Not applicable*
Red check	*Not applicable*	• From 3 strips 2″ wide, cut: 2 pieces 9½″ long 2 pieces 30½″ long
Red	• From 3 strips ¾″ wide, cut: 2 pieces 14″ long 2 pieces 38½″ long	*Not applicable*
Binding	• Cut 3 strips 2″ wide	• Cut 3 strips 2″ wide

QUILT ASSEMBLY

When the blocks in this quilt are arranged together correctly, they form big "Twisty Stars" running down the length of the quilt center. Use the Quilt Assembly chart, diagrams, and project photos to lay out the blocks for the center. Place a plain square in the star centers where there is no letter in the Quilt Assembly chart. Note that all the A Blocks are placed so that the large Position 3 triangles face toward the inside of the star. Sew the blocks together to form the quilt center, and press.

BORDERS FOR 38″ × 14″ RUNNER

1. Use the Borders and Binding chart to prepare the 1¼″-wide lavender inner border strips.

2. Stitch the 2 short inner border pieces to the ends of the quilt and the 2 long pieces to the sides of the quilt. Press to the outside.

3. Repeat Steps 1 and 2 for the ¾″-wide red border.

Quilt assembly diagram, 38″ × 14″

BORDERS FOR 36″ × 18″ RUNNER

1. Use the Borders and Binding chart to prepare the 2″-wide red check inner border strips.

2. Stitch the 2 short inner border pieces to the ends of the quilt and the 2 long pieces to the sides of the quilt. Press toward the border.

3. Stitch 2 short rows of 4 A Blocks together by joining the Position 3 side of one block with the Position 1 side of another block. Stitch these rows to the ends of the quilt.

4. Stitch 2 long rows of 10 A Blocks together in the same fashion. Stitch a 3½″ × 3½″ square of green fabric to each end of the long rows. Stitch to the sides of the quilt. Press toward the inner border.

Quilt assembly diagram, 36″ × 18″

Hugs & Kisses

This quilt reminds me of a magic carpet or a lattice with the light shining through from the back. For this quilt, you have 2 size options: 57″ × 72″ and 68″ × 86″.

FABRIC REQUIREMENTS Yardage is based on 42″-wide fabric unless noted.		
Fabric	**57″ × 72″ Quilt**	**68″ × 86″ Quilt**
Gold	1½ yds	2⅛ yds
Dark blue	1¼ yds	1⅞ yds
Ruby	1⅛ yds	1½ yds
Fuchsia	1 yd	1¼ yds
Orange	¾ yd	1 yd
Burgundy	1 yd	1⅛ yds
Ruby (for binding)	½ yd	⅝ yd
Batting	61″ × 76″	72″ × 90″
108″-wide backing	1¾ yds	2⅛ yds

CUTTING BLOCKS Strips are cut across width of fabric, selvage to selvage.		
Fabric	**57″ × 72″ Quilt**	**68″ × 86″ Quilt**
Gold	• From 7 strips 6½″ wide, cut: 41 squares 6½″ × 6½″	• From 9 strips 7½″ wide, cut: 41 squares 7½″ × 7½″
Dark blue	• From 2 strips 6½″ wide, cut: 12 squares 6½″ × 6½″ • From 4 strips 6″ wide, cut: 23 squares 6″ × 6″	• From 3 strips 7½″ wide, cut: 12 squares 7½″ × 7½″ • From 5 strips 7″ wide, cut: 23 squares 7″ × 7″
Ruby	• From 2 strips 6½″ wide, cut: 10 squares 6½″ × 6½″ 1 square 6″ × 6″ • From 3 strips 6″ wide, cut: 18 squares 6″ × 6″	• From 2 strips 7½″ wide, cut: 10 squares 7½″ × 7½″ • From 4 strips 7″ wide, cut: 19 squares 7″ × 7″
Fuchsia	• From 2 strips 6½″ wide, cut: 8 squares 6½″ × 6½″ 3 squares 6″ × 6″ • From 2 strips 6″ wide, cut: 12 squares 6″ × 6″	• From 2 strips 7½″ wide, cut: 8 squares 7½″ × 7½″ • From 3 strips 7″ wide, cut: 15 squares 7″ × 7″
Orange	• From 1 strip 6½″ wide, cut: 6 squares 6½″ × 6½″ • From 2 strips 6″ wide, cut: 11 squares 6″ × 6″	• From 2 strips 7½″ wide, cut: 6 squares 7½″ × 7½″ 1 square 7″ × 7″ • From 2 strips 7″ wide, cut: 10 squares 7″ × 7″
Burgundy	• From 1 strip 6½″ wide, cut: 5 squares 6½″ × 6½″ • From 2 strips 6″ wide, cut: 9 squares 6″ × 6″	• From 1 strip 7½″ wide, cut: 5 squares 7½″ × 7½″ • From 2 strips 7″ wide, cut: 9 squares 7″ × 7″

BORDERS AND BINDING Strips are cut across width of fabric, selvage to selvage.		
Fabric	**57″ × 72″ Quilt**	**68″ × 86″ Quilt**
Burgundy	• Join 7 strips 1½″ wide; cut: 2 pieces 55½″ long 2 pieces 72½″ long	• Join 8 strips 1½″ wide; cut: 2 pieces 66½″ long 2 pieces 86½″ long
Binding	• Cut 7 strips 2″ wide	• Cut 8 strips 2″ wide

		57″ × 72″ Quilt	68″ × 86″ Quilt
Finished block size		5″ × 5″	6″ × 6″
Position 1 and 2 square size		6½″ × 6½″	7½″ × 7½″
Position 3 square size		6″ × 6″	7″ × 7″
Block A		Make 46 from: 12 Position 1 & 2 23 Position 3 (yields 2 extra 1 & 2 units)	Make 46 from: 12 Position 1 & 2 23 Position 3 (yields 2 extra 1 & 2 units)
Block B		Make 38 from: 10 Position 1 & 2 19 Position 3 (yields 2 extra 1 & 2 units)	Make 38 from: 10 Position 1 & 2 19 Position 3 (yields 2 extra 1 & 2 units)
Block C		Make 30 from: 8 Position 1 & 2 15 Position 3 (yields 2 extra 1 & 2 units)	Make 30 from: 8 Position 1 & 2 15 Position 3 (yields 2 extra 1 & 2 units)
Block D		Make 22 from: 6 Position 1 & 2 11 Position 3 (yields 2 extra 1 & 2 units)	Make 22 from: 6 Position 1 & 2 11 Position 3 (yields 2 extra 1 & 2 units)
Block E		Make 18 from: 5 Position 1 & 2 9 Position 3 (yields 2 extra 1 & 2 units)	Make 18 from: 5 Position 1 & 2 9 Position 3 (yields 2 extra 1 & 2 units)

BLOCK CONSTRUCTION

Always place the gold fabric in Position 1 and use the other color in both Position 2 and Position 3.

QUILT ASSEMBLY

1. Arrange the blocks in concentric rings, using the Quilt Assembly diagram and project photo as guides.

2. Stitch the blocks into rows, pressing alternate rows in opposite directions. Stitch the rows together.

BORDER

1. Use the Borders and Binding chart to prepare the burgundy border strips.

2. Stitch the 2 short border pieces to the top and bottom of the quilt and the 2 long pieces to the sides of the quilt. Press toward the border.

Quilt assembly diagram, 57″ × 72″

Pyramid Color Play 50″ × 70″
2005 Cheryl Malkowski

Pyramid
Color Play

Here is a great quilt to show off your sense of color. There are 14 block colorations and you can have fun blending one block into the next. As you select fabric, think about the order of the color wheel. If you have a hard time choosing all the colors at once, just start by making the A blocks; lay them out and then choose the fabrics for the B blocks. Go on to the next block after you finish the previous one.

FABRIC REQUIREMENTS Yardage is based on 42″-wide fabric unless noted.

Blues and greens make up the most blocks, so keep that in mind as you choose your color combinations. Select 14 light fat quarters, paired with 14 related dark fat quarters. Of the 3 color combinations you want to use the most in the quilt, buy 1 extra fat quarter of each dark.

Fabric	Amount
Light colors for Position 1	Think color wheel! 14 fat quarters
Black for Position 2	1½ yds
Dark colors for Position 3	Pair these up with light Position 1 fabrics. 17 fat quarters
Black (for binding)	½ yd
Batting	54″ × 74″
108″-wide backing	1⅝ yds

CUTTING AND BLOCK CONSTRUCTION

Sketch numbered blocks and glue small pieces of fabric to them to remind you of your color placement. Follow the directions for making Y Blocks on pages 5–9.

	# Position 1, cut 6½″ × 6½″ Light color	# Position 2, cut 6½″ × 6½″ Black (37 total squares needed)	# Position 3, cut 6″ × 6″ Dark color	Total to make of each block
Block A	1	1	2	4
Block B	2	2	4	8
Block C	2	2	4	8
Block D	2	2	4	8
Block E	3	3	6	12
Block F	3	3	6	12
Block G	4	4	8	16

CUTTING AND BLOCK CONSTRUCTION CONTINUED

Sketch numbered blocks and glue small pieces of fabric to them to remind you of your color placement. Follow the directions for making Y Blocks on pages 5–9.

	# Position 1, cut 6½" × 6½" Light color	# Position 2, cut 6½" × 6½" Black (37 total squares needed)	# Position 3, cut 6" × 6" Dark color	Total to make of each block
Block H	5	5	10	20
Block I	3	3	6	12
Block J	4	4	8	16
Block K	3	3	6	12
Block L	2	2	4	8
Block M	1	1	2	4
Block N	2	2	4	7

QUILT ASSEMBLY

Row 1	A	A	B	B	C	D	D	E	F	G	
Row 2	A	A	B	B	C	D	E	E	F	G	H
Row 3	B	B	C	C	D	E	F	F	G	H	
Row 4	B	B	C	D	E	F	F	G	G	H	I
Row 5	C	C	D	E	F	F	G	H	H	I	

Row 6	C	D	E	F	F	G	H	H	I	I	I
Row 7	D	E	F	F	G	H	H	I	I	I	
Row 8	E	E	E	G	G	H	H	I	J	J	K
Row 9	E	G	G	H	H	I	J	J	K	K	
Row 10	G	G	G	H	I	J	J	K	K	L	L
Row 11	G	H	H	I	J	J	K	L	L	M	
Row 12	H	H	H	J	J	K	L	L	M	N	N
Row 13	H	J	J	K	K	K	L	M	N	N	
Row 14	J	J	J	J	K	K	L	M	N	N	N

QUILT ASSEMBLY

1. Using the Quilt Assembly chart, diagram, and project photo as guides, place the blocks according to your own vision for the quilt. The project quilt is arranged according to the color wheel. Note that all the even-numbered rows have 11 blocks, 1 block more than the odd-numbered rows. Cut off 2½″ from each end of the even-numbered rows.

2½″   2½″

Trim 2½″ from each end of the even-numbered rows.

2. Stitch the horizontal rows together and press the seam allowances to one side. Then stitch the rows together to complete the quilt center. Press.

3. Cut 7 black 2″-wide strips for binding.

Quilt assembly diagram

Twisty Star Trellis 57″ × 72″

2005 Cheryl Malkowski

Twisty Star Trellis

Here's a very traditional look for this versatile little block. I especially like the effect of the pieced border. It's almost like having prairie points without all the extra work.

For this quilt, there is only one size option given. The finished block size is 3″ × 3″ and the finished quilt size is 57″ × 72″.

FABRIC REQUIREMENTS Yardage is based on 42"-wide fabric unless noted.	
Fabric	Amount
Red	$1\frac{5}{8}$ yds
Light beige	$\frac{1}{2}$ yd
Gold	$1\frac{1}{8}$ yds
Green floral	$3\frac{1}{4}$ yds
Red (for binding)	$\frac{1}{2}$ yd
Batting	61" × 76"
108"-wide backing	$1\frac{3}{4}$ yds

CUTTING BLOCKS Strips are cut across width of fabric, selvage to selvage.	
Fabric	57" × 72" Quilt
Red	• From 4 strips $4\frac{1}{2}$" wide, cut: 32 squares $4\frac{1}{2}$" × $4\frac{1}{2}$" • From 1 strip 4" wide, cut: 2 squares 4" × 4" 1 square $3\frac{1}{2}$" × $3\frac{1}{2}$" • From 1 strip $3\frac{1}{2}$" wide, cut: 11 squares $3\frac{1}{2}$" × $3\frac{1}{2}$"
Light beige	• From 2 strips $4\frac{1}{2}$" wide, cut: 12 squares $4\frac{1}{2}$" × $4\frac{1}{2}$" • From 2 strips $1\frac{1}{2}$" wide, cut: 31 squares $1\frac{1}{2}$" × $1\frac{1}{2}$"
Green floral	• From 2 strips 18" wide, cut: 3 squares 18" × 18", then cut each diagonally twice for side triangles (yields 2 extra side triangles) 2 squares $9\frac{1}{2}$" × $9\frac{1}{2}$" • From 1 strip 12" wide, cut: 2 squares 12" × 12", then cut each diagonally once for corner triangles • From 1 strip $9\frac{1}{2}$" wide, cut: 4 squares $9\frac{1}{2}$" × $9\frac{1}{2}$" • From 3 strips $4\frac{1}{2}$" wide, cut: 20 squares $4\frac{1}{2}$" × $4\frac{1}{2}$" • From 7 strips 4" wide, cut: 65 squares 4" × 4"
Gold	• From 5 strips $3\frac{1}{2}$" wide, cut: 48 squares $3\frac{1}{2}$" × $3\frac{1}{2}$"

BORDERS, SASHING AND BINDING Strips are cut across width of fabric, selvage to selvage.	
Fabric	57" × 72" Quilt
Red	• From 12 strips $1\frac{1}{2}$" wide, cut: 48 pieces $9\frac{1}{2}$" long (sashing) • Join 6 strips $1\frac{1}{2}$" wide; cut: 2 pieces $49\frac{1}{2}$" long 2 pieces $66\frac{1}{2}$" long
Gold	• Join 6 strips $2\frac{3}{4}$" wide; cut: 2 pieces 45" long 2 pieces $64\frac{1}{2}$" long
Binding	• Cut 7 strips 2" wide

BLOCK CONSTRUCTION

Sketch numbered blocks and glue small pieces of fabric to them to remind you of your color placement. Follow the directions for making Y Blocks on pages 5–9.

	57″ × 72″ Quilt
Finished block size	3″ × 3″
Position 1 & 2 square size	4½″ × 4½″
Position 3 square size	4″ × 4″
Block A	Make 48 from: 12 Position 1 & 2 24 Position 3
Block B	Make 78 from: 20 Position 1 & 2 39 Position 3 (yields 2 extra 1 & 2 units)
Block C	Make 4 from: 2 green 4″ × 4″ squares & 2 red 4″ × 4″ squares; trim to 3½″ × 3½″

BLOCK CONSTRUCTION

The A Blocks will be used in the Twisty Star blocks, and the B Blocks will be in the pieced border.

BLOCK C

The C Block is made with 2 half-square triangles. Place 4″ × 4″ squares of green print and red right sides together. Cut once diagonally from corner to corner. Stitch ¼″ from the bias edge. Use Clip & Flip Pressing by clipping the seam allowance in the center and pressing counterclockwise from the back. Trim the block to 3½″ × 3½″. Make 4 blocks. These will be used in the pieced border.

QUILT ASSEMBLY

1. Arrange A Blocks together in 3-by-3 squares to form 12 Twisty Star blocks. Each Twisty Star block uses 4 A Blocks, 4 gold 3½″ × 3½″ squares, and 1 red center 3½″ × 3½″ square. Note that all the A Blocks are placed so that the large triangle of Position 3 faces toward the inside of the star. Press toward the plain squares. These completed blocks should measure 9½″ × 9½″.

Twisty Star block

2. The Borders, Sashing, and Binding chart gives the cutting information for the sashing. Use the Quilt Assembly diagram and project photo as guides to arrange diagonal rows of setting triangles, sashing, blocks, and cornerstones. Sew the rows together and press the seams toward the sashing.

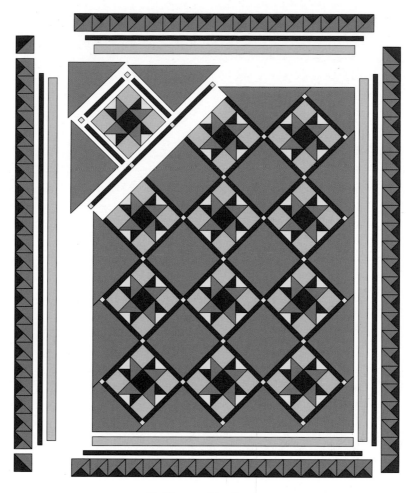

Quilt assembly diagram

3. Stitch the rows of the quilt together to finish the quilt center. Note that the setting triangles are purposely extra large so that your blocks will "float" (not come all the way to the edge).

4. Cut the quilt center to 45″ × 60″, being sure to leave roughly the same amount of background on all sides, centering the blocks.

BORDERS

1. Use the Borders, Sashing, and Binding chart to prepare the 2³/₄″-wide gold inner border strips.

2. Stitch the 2 short inner border pieces to the top and bottom of the quilt and the 2 long pieces to the sides of the quilt. Press toward the outside.

3. Repeat Steps 1 and 2 for the 1½″-wide red border strips.

4. Make 2 rows with 17 B Blocks each for the outer border. Note that the Position 2 triangle is never in the joining seams of the blocks. Press to one side. Stitch these border rows to the top and bottom of the quilt with the Position 2 triangle facing away from the quilt center. Press the seams toward the quilt center.

5. In the same manner as above, stitch 2 rows with 22 B Blocks each for the side border rows. To the end of each row, add a C Block, noting the color placement in the photo. Stitch these rows to the sides of the quilt and press toward the center.

Triangles All Around

Compare this quilt with *Floral Triangles All Around* on page 58 to see how different this same pattern looks done in French country style. Have fun varying the colors within a block as I did using 2 different light greens in the E & F Blocks.

For this quilt, there is only one size option given. The finished block size is 6″ × 6″ and the finished quilt size is 70½″ × 70½″.

FABRIC REQUIREMENTS Yardage is based on 42″-wide fabric unless noted.	
Fabric	**Amount**
Gold	$^5/_8$ yd
Fuchsia	$^5/_8$ yd
Dark green	$^7/_8$ yd
Bright blue	$^5/_8$ yd
Purple	$^5/_8$ yd
Green	1 yd
Blue	$^5/_8$ yd
Yellow	$^5/_8$ yd
Light green	$^7/_8$ yd
Pale yellow	$^1/_2$ yd
Pale green	$^1/_2$ yd
Aqua	$^5/_8$ yd
Fuchsia (for inner border)	$^3/_8$ yd
Gold (for middle border)	$^1/_4$ yd
Blue (for outer border)	1 yd
Purple (for binding)	$^5/_8$ yd
Batting	75″ × 75″
108″-wide backing	$2^1/_8$ yds

CUTTING BLOCKS Strips are cut across width of fabric, selvage to selvage.	
Fabric	**$70^1/_2″$ × $70^1/_2″$ Quilt**
Gold	• From 2 strips $7^1/_2″$ wide, cut: 6 squares $7^1/_2″$ × $7^1/_2″$
Fuchsia	• From 2 strips $7^1/_2″$ wide, cut: 6 squares $7^1/_2″$ × $7^1/_2″$
Dark green	• From 3 strips 7″ wide, cut: 12 squares 7″ × 7″
Bright blue	• From 2 strips $7^1/_2″$ wide, cut: 10 squares $7^1/_2″$ × $7^1/_2″$
Purple	• From 2 strips $7^1/_2″$ wide, cut: 10 squares $7^1/_2″$ × $7^1/_2″$
Green	• From 4 strips 7″ wide, cut: 18 squares 7″ × 7″
Blue	• From 2 strips $7^1/_2″$ wide, cut: 8 squares $7^1/_2″$ × $7^1/_2″$
Yellow	• From 2 strips $7^1/_2″$ wide, cut: 8 squares $7^1/_2″$ × $7^1/_2″$
Light green	• From 3 strips 7″ wide, cut: 14 squares 7″ × 7″
Pale yellow	• From 1 strip $7^1/_2″$ wide, cut: 4 squares $7^1/_2″$ × $7^1/_2″$
Pale green	• From 1 strip $7^1/_2″$ wide, cut: 4 squares $7^1/_2″$ × $7^1/_2″$
Aqua	• From 2 strips 7″ wide, cut: 6 squares 7″ × 7″

Sketch numbered blocks and glue small pieces of fabric to them to remind you of your color placement. Follow the directions for making Y Blocks on pages 5–9.

	$70\frac{1}{2}'' \times 70\frac{1}{2}''$ Quilt
Finished block size	$6'' \times 6''$
Position 1 & 2 square size	$7\frac{1}{2}'' \times 7\frac{1}{2}''$
Position 3 square size	$7'' \times 7''$
Block A	Make 12 from: 3 Position 1 & 2 6 Position 3
Block B	Make 12 from: 3 Position 1 & 2 6 Position 3
Block C	Make 18 from: 5 Position 1 & 2 9 Position 3 (yields 2 extra 1 & 2 units)
Block D	Make 18 from: 5 Position 1 & 2 9 Position 3 (yields 2 extra 1 & 2 units)
Block E	Make 14 from: 4 Position 1 & 2 7 Position 3 (yields 2 extra 1 & 2 units)
Block F	Make 14 from: 4 Position 1 & 2 7 Position 3 (yields 2 extra 1 & 2 units)
Block G	Make 6 from: 2 Position 1 & 2 3 Position 3 (yields 2 extra 1 & 2 units)
Block H	Make 6 from: 2 Position 1 & 2 3 Position 3 (yields 2 extra 1 & 2 units)

QUILT ASSEMBLY

Row 1	G	G	E	E	C	D	F	F	H	H
Row 2	G	E	E	C	C	D	D	F	F	H
Row 3	E	E	C	C	A	B	D	D	F	F
Row 4	E	C	C	A	A	B	B	D	D	F
Row 5	C	C	A	A	A	B	B	B	D	D
Row 6	D	D	B	B	B	A	A	A	C	C
Row 7	F	D	D	B	B	A	A	C	C	E
Row 8	F	F	D	D	B	A	C	C	E	E
Row 9	H	F	F	D	D	C	C	E	E	G
Row 10	H	H	F	F	D	C	E	E	G	G

BORDERS AND BINDING
Strips are cut across width of fabric, selvage to selvage.

Fabric	70½" × 70½" Quilt
Fuchsia	• Join 7 strips 1½" wide; cut: 2 pieces 60½" long 2 pieces 62½" long
Gold	• Join 7 strips ¾" wide; cut: 2 pieces 62½" long 2 pieces 63" long
Blue	• Join 7 strips 4½" wide; cut: 2 pieces 63" long 2 pieces 71" long
Binding	• Cut 8 strips 2" wide

Quilt assembly diagram

BLOCK CONSTRUCTION

Note that the Position 1 and Position 2 fabrics reverse while the Position 3 fabric remains the same in block sets A & B, C & D, E & F, and G & H. Place each block type in its own zippered bag to keep everything in order while you work.

QUILT ASSEMBLY

1. Assemble the rows using the Quilt Assembly chart, diagram, and the project photo as guides. Alternate the pressing direction for each row.

2. Stitch the rows together and press the seams to one side to complete the quilt center.

BORDERS

1. Use the Borders and Binding chart to prepare the 1½"-wide fuchsia inner border strips. Cut the strips according to the chart or match the measurements of your quilt center.

2. Stitch the 2 short inner border pieces to the top and bottom of the quilt and the 2 long pieces to the sides of the quilt. Press toward the outside.

3. Repeat Steps 1 and 2 for the ¾"-wide gold border strips and the 4½"-wide blue border strips.

Scrappy Sunshine & Stars

This cheerful quilt works great in other colors, too, where the sunshine and stars become flowers. Check out *Jenny's Garden* on page 61. It's the same pattern using unlikely colors inspired by my friend's corner garden.

For this quilt, there is only one size option given. The finished block size is 4½″ × 4½″ and the finished quilt size is 58½″ × 58½″. For a scrappy look, use 9 fat quarters in a variety of medium and dark blues.

FABRIC REQUIREMENTS Yardage is based on 42″-wide fabric unless noted.	
Fabric	**Amount**
Dark and medium blues	9 fat quarters
Pale yellow	$3/4$ yd
Yellow	$3/8$ yd
Gold	1 yd
Light blue	$1 1/4$ yds
Blue (for binding)	$1/2$ yd
Batting	63″ × 63″
108″-wide backing	$1 3/4$ yds

CUTTING BLOCKS Strips are cut across width of fabric, selvage to selvage.	
Fabric	**$58^{1/2}″ × 58^{1/2}″$ Quilt**
Dark and medium blues	• From the fat quarters, cut: 24 squares 6″ × 6″ 40 squares $5^{1/2}″ × 5^{1/2}″$ 9 squares 5″ × 5″ (1 from each fat quarter)
Pale yellow	• From 3 strips 6″ wide, cut: 13 squares 6″ × 6″ 2 squares $5^{1/2}″ × 5^{1/2}″$
Yellow	• From 1 strip 6″ wide, cut: 2 squares 6″ × 6″ 4 squares $5^{1/2}″ × 5^{1/2}″$
Gold	• From 1 strip 6″ wide, cut: 2 squares 6″ × 6″ 4 squares $5^{1/2}″ × 5^{1/2}″$ • From 1 strip 5″ wide, cut: 4 squares 5″ × 5″
Light blue	• From 3 strips 6″ wide, cut: 15 squares 6″ × 6″ • From 2 strips $5^{1/2}″$ wide, cut: 10 squares $5^{1/2}″ × 5^{1/2}″$

BORDERS AND BINDING Strips are cut across width of fabric, selvage to selvage.	
Fabric	**$58^{1/2}″ × 58^{1/2}″$ Quilt**
Light blue	• Join 5 strips 2″ wide; cut: 2 pieces 41″ long 2 pieces 44″ long
Gold	• Join 5 strips $3^{1/2}″$ wide; cut: 2 pieces 44″ long 2 pieces 50″ long
Binding	• Cut 7 strips 2″ wide

BLOCK CONSTRUCTION Use Clip & Flip Pressing.
Sketch numbered blocks and glue small pieces of fabric to them to remind you of your color placement.
Follow the directions for making Y Blocks on pages 5–9.

	$58\frac{1}{2}'' \times 58\frac{1}{2}''$ **Quilt**
Finished block size	$4\frac{1}{2}'' \times 4\frac{1}{2}''$
Position 1 & 2 square size	$6'' \times 6''$
Position 3 square size	$5\frac{1}{2}'' \times 5\frac{1}{2}''$
Block A	Make 36 from: 9 Position 1 & 2 (1 from each fat quarter) 18 Position 3 (2 from each fat quarter)
Block B	Make 4 from: 1 Position 1 & 2 2 Position 3
Block C	Make 4 from: 1 Position 1 & 2 2 Position 3
Block D	Make 4 from: 1 Position 1 & 2 2 Position 3
Block E	Make 4 from: 1 Position 1 & 2 2 Position 3
Block F	Make 8 from: 2 Position 1 & 2 4 Position 3
Block G	Make 8 from: 2 Position 1 & 2 4 Position 3
Block H	Make 44 from: 11 Position 1 & 2 22 Position 3
Block I	Make 4 from: 2 pale yellow $5\frac{1}{2}'' \times 5\frac{1}{2}''$ squares & 2 light blue $5\frac{1}{2}'' \times 5\frac{1}{2}''$ squares; trim to $5'' \times 5''$

QUILT ASSEMBLY									
Row 1	I	A	F	G	A	F	G	A	I
Row 2	A		A	A		A	A		A
Row 3	G	A	B	C	A	D	E	A	F
Row 4	F	A	C	B	A	E	D	A	G
Row 5	A		A	A		A	A		A
Row 6	G	A	D	E	A	B	C	A	F
Row 7	F	A	E	D	A	C	B	A	G
Row 8	A		A	A		A	A		A
Row 9	I	A	G	F	A	G	F	A	I

BLOCK CONSTRUCTION

Note: For the H Block only, there is no need to use Clip & Flip Pressing; just press toward Position 3 on the second pressing.

BLOCK I

The I Block is made with 2 half-square triangles. Place 5½″ × 5½″ squares of light blue and pale yellow right sides together. Cut once diagonally from corner to corner. Stitch ¼″ from the bias edge. Use Clip & Flip Pressing by snipping the seam allowance in the center and pressing counterclockwise from the back side. Trim the block to 5″ × 5″. Make 4 blocks. These blocks will be used in the quilt center corners.

QUILT ASSEMBLY

1. Lay out the blocks using the Quilt Assembly chart, diagram, and project photo as guides for placement and block orientation. Place a 5″ × 5″ square in the star centers where there is no letter in the Quilt Assembly chart. Stitch the blocks into rows and press in alternating directions.

2. Stitch the rows together to complete the quilt center. Press the seam allowances to one side.

BORDERS

1. Use the Borders and Binding chart to prepare the 2″-wide light blue inner border strips.

2. Stitch the 2 short inner border pieces to the top and bottom of the quilt and the 2 long pieces to the sides of the quilt. Press toward the border.

3. Repeat Steps 1 and 2 for the 3½″-wide gold middle border strips.

4. Stitch 4 rows of 11 H Blocks together for the outer border. Make adjustments as necessary to ensure that this outer pieced border matches the size of the quilt center. Stitch the outer border to the top and bottom of the quilt.

5. Stitch a 5″ × 5″ gold square to each end of the remaining 2 H Block borders and stitch them to the sides of the quilt. Press toward the inner border.

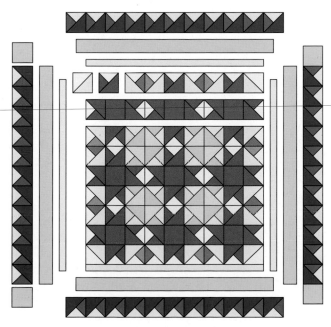

Quilt assembly diagram

Twisted Ribbons 68″ × 86″

2006 Cheryl Malkowski
Pieced by Pat Glass. Quilted by Jane Yurk.

Twisted Ribbons

Time to celebrate with this party quilt!

For this quilt, you have 2 size options: 57″ × 72″ and 68″ × 86″.

FABRIC REQUIREMENTS Yardage is based on 42"-wide fabric unless noted.

Fabric	57" × 72" Quilt	68" × 86" Quilt
Black	1½ yds	2 yds
Dark value	Fat ⅛ or ¼ yd (per vertical row)	Fat or regular ¼ yd (per vertical row)
Medium value	Fat or regular ¼ yd (per vertical row)	Fat or regular ¼ yd (per vertical row)
Yellow	⅜ yd	⅜ yd
Purple print	1 yd	1¼ yds
Purple (for binding)	½ yd	⅝ yd
Batting	61" × 76"	72" × 90"
108"-wide backing	1¾ yds	2 yds

CUTTING BLOCKS Strips are cut across width of fabric, selvage to selvage.

Fabric	57" × 72" Quilt	68" × 86" Quilt
Black	• From 5 strips 6½" wide, cut: 27 squares 6½" × 6½"	• From 6 strips 7½" wide, cut: 27 squares 7½" × 7½"
Dark value	• For each vertical row, cut: 3 squares 6½" × 6½"	• For each vertical row, cut: 3 squares 7½" × 7½"
Medium value	• For each vertical row, cut: 6 squares 6" × 6"	• For each vertical row, cut: 6 squares 7" × 7"

BLOCK CONSTRUCTION Use Clip & Flip Pressing.

See special instructions for color placement for the A and B Blocks on page 40. Follow the directions for making Y Blocks on pages 5–9.

	57" × 72" Quilt	68" × 86" Quilt
Finished block size	5" × 5"	6" × 6"
Position 1 & 2 square size	6½" × 6½"	7½" × 7½"
Position 3 square size	6" × 6"	7" × 7"
Block A 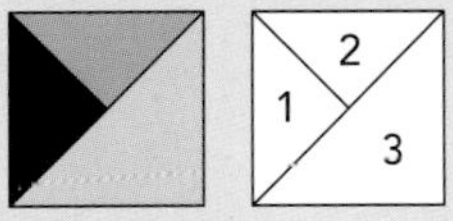	For each color— Make 12 from: 3 Position 1 & 2 6 Position 3	For each color— Make 12 from: 3 Position 1 & 2 6 Position 3
Block B 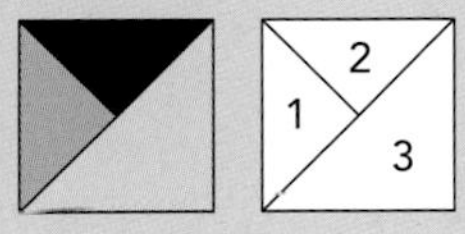	For each color— Make 12 from: 3 Position 1 & 2 6 Position 3	For each color— Make 12 from: 3 Position 1 & 2 6 Position 3

BORDERS AND BINDING Strips are cut across width of fabric, selvage to selvage.		
Fabric	**57″ × 72″ Quilt**	**68″ × 86″ Quilt**

Black	• Join 6 strips 2″ wide; cut:
	  2 pieces 45½″ long
	  2 pieces 63½″ long
		• Join 7 strips 2½″ wide; cut:
		  2 pieces 54½″ long
		  2 pieces 76½″ long

Yellow	• Join 6 strips 1½″ wide; cut:
	  2 pieces 48½″ long
	  2 pieces 65½″ long
		• Join 7 strips 1½″ wide; cut:
		  2 pieces 58½″ long
		  2 pieces 78½″ long

Purple print	• Join 7 strips 4″ wide; cut:
	  2 pieces 50½″ long
	  2 pieces 72½″ long
		• Join 8 strips 4½″ wide; cut:
		  2 pieces 60½″ long
		  2 pieces 86½″ long

Binding	• Cut 7 strips 2″ wide	• Cut 9 strips 2″ wide

BLOCK CONSTRUCTION

The *Twisted Ribbons* Block Construction chart has the Y Blocks only shaded to show you where the color values go in each block. Decide which colors to use in each row, stack each row together, and number them as Row 1 through Row 9.

The even-numbered rows have fabrics in positions different than the odd-numbered rows, so separate the squares into 2 piles: Rows 1, 3, 5, 7, and 9 are made with all A Blocks. Rows 2, 4, 6, and 8 are made with all B Blocks.

Use the diagrams below to plan the color arrangement for your quilt.

BLOCK A (ROWS 1, 3, 5, 7, AND 9)

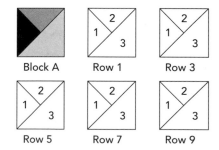

1. For each row, make 12 Position 1 and Position 2 triangle units. Put black fabric in Position 1 and put a dark-value fabric in Position 2.

2. Use 6 related medium-value squares for Position 3.

3. Add Position 3 to the pieced Position 1 and Position 2 units. Repeat Steps 1 and 2 to make a total of 60 A Blocks, 12 for each odd-numbered row.

BLOCK B (ROWS 2, 4, 6, AND 8)

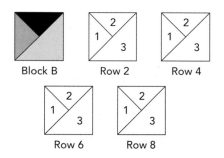

1. For each row, make 12 Position 1 and Position 2 triangle units. Put a dark-value fabric in Position 1 and put black in Position 2.

2. Use 6 related medium-value squares for Position 3.

3. Add Position 3 to the pieced Position 1 and Position 2 units. Repeat Steps 1 and 2 to make a total of 48 B Blocks, 12 for each even-numbered row.

QUILT ASSEMBLY

1. Stitch each *vertical* row together using the Quilt Assembly diagram and project photo as guides for color placement. Press the seams on the odd rows down and the even rows up.

2. Stitch the rows together and press the seams to one side to complete the quilt center.

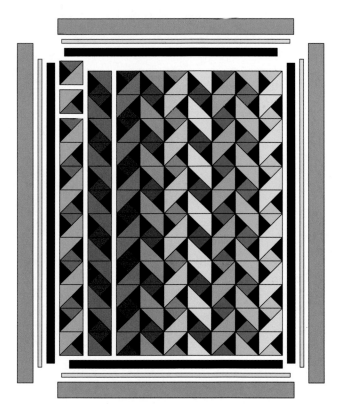

Quilt assembly diagram

BORDERS

1. Use the Borders and Binding chart to prepare the black inner border strips.

2. Stitch the 2 short inner border pieces to the top and bottom of the quilt and the 2 long pieces to the sides of the quilt. Press toward the outside.

3. Repeat Steps 1 and 2 for the yellow middle border and the purple print outer border.

Lacy Pinwheels

The edges of the quilt center remind me of paper snowflake cutouts like we made in elementary school. I love how the big pinwheels "borrow" a point from the smaller squares. This design works best with a strong contrast between colors.

For this quilt, you have 2 size options: 54″ × 54″ and 78″ × 102″.

FABRIC REQUIREMENTS Yardage is based on 42"-wide fabric unless noted.

Fabric	54" × 54" Quilt	78" × 102" Quilt
Black	$1^7/8$ yds	$4^1/8$ yds
Multi-print	$1^3/8$ yds	$3^7/8$ yds
Fuchsia	1 yd	$3^3/4$ yds
Black (for binding)	$^1/2$ yd	$^3/4$ yd
Batting	58" × 58"	82" × 106"
108"-wide backing	$1^5/8$ yds	$2^1/3$ yds

CUTTING BLOCKS Strips are cut across width of fabric, selvage to selvage.

Fabric	54" × 54" Quilt	78" × 102" Quilt
Black	• From 1 strip $7^1/2$" wide, cut: 5 squares $7^1/2$" × $7^1/2$" • From 4 strips $4^1/2$" wide, cut: 28 squares $4^1/2$" × $4^1/2$" 2 squares 4" × 4"	• From 4 strips $7^1/2$" wide, cut: 18 squares $7^1/2$" × $7^1/2$" • From 12 strips $4^1/2$" wide, cut: 93 squares $4^1/2$" × $4^1/2$" 2 squares 4" × 4"
Multi-print	• From 1 strip $7^1/2$" wide, cut: 5 squares $7^1/2$" × $7^1/2$" • From 4 strips $4^1/2$" wide, cut: 28 squares $4^1/2$" × $4^1/2$" • From 3 strips 4" wide, cut: 22 squares 4" × 4"	• From 4 strips $7^1/2$" wide, cut: 18 squares $7^1/2$" × $7^1/2$" • From 12 strips $4^1/2$" wide, cut: 93 squares $4^1/2$" × $4^1/2$" • From 5 strips 4" wide, cut: 43 squares 4" × 4"
Fuchsia	• From 2 strips 7" wide, cut: 10 squares 7" × 7" • From 4 strips 4" wide, cut: 36 squares 4" × 4"	• From 8 strips 7" wide, cut: 36 squares 7" × 7" • From 15 strips 4" wide, cut: 143 squares 4" × 4"

BLOCK CONSTRUCTION

Sketch numbered blocks and glue small pieces of fabric to them to remind you of your color placement. Follow the directions for making Y Blocks on pages 5–9.

	54" × 54" Quilt	78" × 102" Quilt
Finished Block A size	6" × 6"	6" × 6"
Position 1 & 2 square size for A	$7^1/2$" × $7^1/2$"	$7^1/2$" × $7^1/2$"
Position 3 square size for A	7" × 7"	7" × 7"
Block A	Make 20 from: 5 Position 1 & 2 10 Position 3	Make 72 from: 18 Position 1 & 2 36 Position 3

Sketch numbered blocks and glue small pieces of fabric to them to remind you of your color placement. Follow the directions for making Y Blocks on pages 5–9.

	54″ × 54″ Quilt	78″ × 102″ Quilt
Finished Block B & C size	3″ × 3″	3″ × 3″
Position 1 & 2 square size for B & C	4½″ × 4½″	4½″ × 4½″
Position 3 square size for B & C	4″ × 4″	4″ × 4″
Block B	Make 72 from: 18 Position 1 & 2 36 Position 3	Make 286 from: 72 Position 1 & 2 143 Position 3
Block C	Make 40 from: 10 Position 1 & 2 20 Position 3	Make 82 from: 21 Position 1 & 2 41 Position 3 (yields 2 extra 1 & 2 units)
Block D	Make 4 from: 2 black 4″ × 4″ squares & 2 multi-print 4″ × 4″ squares; trim to 3½″ × 3½″	Make 4 from: 2 black 4″ × 4″ squares & 2 multi-print 4″ × 4″ squares; trim to 3½″ × 3½″

BLOCK BORDERS

	54″ × 54″ Quilt	78″ × 102″ Quilt
Blocks per row	• Top and bottom, each: 10 C Blocks, 2 B Blocks	• Top and bottom, each: 17 C Blocks, 3 B Blocks
	• Each side: 10 C Blocks, 2 B Blocks, plus 2 D Blocks	• Each side: 24 C Blocks, 4 B Blocks, plus 2 D Blocks

BORDERS AND BINDING Strips are cut across width of fabric, selvage to selvage.

Fabric	54″ × 54″ Quilt	78″ × 102″ Quilt
Black	• Join 6 strips 3½″ wide; cut: 2 pieces 48½″ long (outer) 2 pieces 54½″ long • Join 5 strips 2½″ wide; cut: 2 pieces 42½″ long (inner) 2 pieces 46½″ long	• Join 9 strips 3½″ wide; cut: 2 pieces 72½″ long (outer) 2 pieces 102½″ long • Join 9 strips 2½″ wide; cut: 2 pieces 66½″ long (inner) 2 pieces 94½″ long
Multi-print	• Join 5 strips 1½″ wide; cut: 2 pieces 46½″ long (middle) 2 pieces 48½″ long	• Join 9 strips 1½″ wide; cut: 2 pieces 70½″ long (middle) 2 pieces 96½″ long
Binding	• Cut 6 strips 2″ wide	• Cut 10 strips 2″ wide

BLOCK CONSTRUCTION

To achieve the desired visual effect in this quilt, there are 2 very different block sizes. The A Block is 6″ × 6″ when finished, and the B Block and C Block are 3″ × 3″ when finished.

BLOCK D

The D Block is made with 2 half-square triangles. Place 4″ × 4″ squares of black and multi-print fabrics right sides together. Cut once diagonally from corner to corner. Stitch ¼″ from the bias edge. Press toward the multi-print fabric. Trim to 3½″ × 3½″. Make 4 blocks. Set aside to use in the pieced border corners.

QUILT ASSEMBLY

1. Arrange and stitch together the A Block units in groups of 4 to make large Whirlwind blocks that measure 12½″ × 12½″. Press toward the Position 3 fabric, clipping where necessary. Make 5 for the 54″ × 54″ quilt and 18 for the 78″ × 102″ quilt.

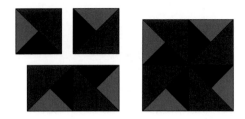

Whirlwind B Block, 6½″ × 6½″

2. Set aside 8 B Blocks for the pieced border (14 for the larger-sized quilt).

3. Arrange and stitch together the remaining B Blocks in groups of 4 to make small Whirlwind blocks that measure 6½″ × 6½″. Press toward the Position 3 fabric, clipping where necessary. Make 16 for the smaller quilt and 68 for the larger quilt.

4. Arrange and stitch together the small Whirlwind blocks made from the B Block in groups of 4. This unit measures 12½″ × 12½″. Press toward the Position 3 fabric, clipping where necessary. Make 4 for the smaller quilt and 17 for the larger quilt.

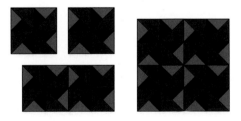

Whirlwind B block unit, 12½″ × 12½″

5. Stitch the rows together using the Quilt Assembly diagram and project photo as guides for block placement, alternating large and small Whirlwind block units. Press the rows in alternating directions. The larger size has 7 horizontal rows of 5 alternating blocks.

6. Stitch the rows together to complete the quilt center. Press.

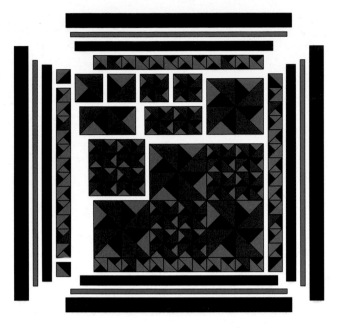

Quilt assembly diagram, 54″ × 54″

BORDERS

1. Refer to the Block Borders chart for the number of blocks for each row.

2. Stitch the blocks into rows. Stitch them to the top and bottom of the quilt, nesting the seams as you go and press the long seam allowance to one side. Then add the border rows to the sides of the quilt.

3. Use the Borders and Binding chart to prepare the 2½″-wide black inner border strips. Cut the strips according to the chart or match the measurements of your quilt center.

4. Stitch the 2 short inner border pieces to the top and bottom of the quilt and the 2 long pieces to the sides of the quilt. Press to the outside.

5. Repeat Steps 3 and 4 for the 1½″-wide multi-print middle border strips and the 3½″-wide black outer border strips. Press.

2005 Cheryl Malkowski

Giant Whirligig

When choosing fabrics for this quilt, remember that for best results, there needs to be a lot of contrast to get the whirling effect. Think in terms of a dark fabric in Position 1, a light fabric in Position 2, and a related medium allover print in Position 3.

For this quilt, you have 3 size options: 46″ × 46″, 68″ × 68″, and 86″ × 98″.

FABRIC REQUIREMENTS Yardage is based on 42"-wide fabric unless noted.

Fabric	46" × 46" Quilt	68" × 68" Quilt	86" × 98" Quilt
Green (dark)	1½ yds	2½ yds	4 yds
Pink (light)	¾ yd	1½ yds	2¼ yds
Print (medium)	1¼ yds	2¼ yds	3½ yds
Green (for binding)	⅜ yd	½ yd	¾ yd
Batting	50" × 50"	72" × 72"	90" × 102"
108"-wide backing	1⅜ yds	2 yds	2⅝ yds

CUTTING BLOCKS Strips are cut across width of fabric, selvage to selvage.

Fabric	46" × 46" Quilt	68" × 68" Quilt	86" × 98" Quilt
Green	• From 3 strips 5½" wide, cut: 21 squares 5½" × 5½" • From 1 strip 5" wide, cut: 2 squares 5" × 5" 1 square 4½" × 4½"	• From 6 strips 6½" wide, cut: 31 squares 6½" × 6½" 2 squares 6" × 6" 1 square 5½" × 5½"	• From 8 strips 7½" wide, cut: 37 squares 7½" × 7½" 2 squares 7" × 7" 1 square 6½" × 6½"
Pink	• From 3 strips 5½" wide, cut: 18 squares 5½" × 5½"	• From 5 strips 6½" wide, cut: 27 squares 6½" × 6½"	• From 7 strips 7½" wide, cut: 32 squares 7½" × 7½"
Print	• From 1 strip 5½" wide, cut: 3 squares 5½" × 5½" • From 6 strips 5" wide, cut: 44 squares 5" × 5"	• From 1 strip 6½" wide, cut: 4 squares 6½" × 6½" • From 11 strips 6" wide, cut: 64 squares 6" × 6"	• From 1 strip 7½" wide, cut: 5 squares 7½" × 7½" • From 15 strips 7" wide, cut: 75 squares 7" × 7"

BLOCK CONSTRUCTION Use Clip & Flip Pressing.

Sketch numbered blocks and glue small pieces of fabric to them to remind you of your color placement. Follow the directions for making Y Blocks on pages 5–9.

	46" × 46" Quilt	68" × 68" Quilt	86" × 98" Quilt
Finished block size	4" × 4"	5" × 5"	6" × 6"
Position 1 & 2 square size	5½" × 5½"	6½" × 6½"	7½" × 7½"
Position 3 square size	5" × 5"	6" × 6"	7" × 7"
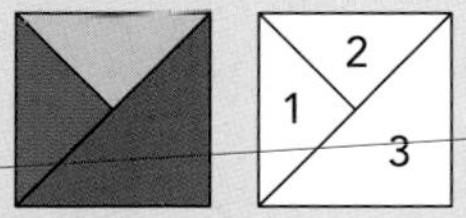 Block A	Make 72 from: 18 Position 1 & 2 36 Position 3	Make 108 from: 27 Position 1 & 2 54 Position 3	Make 128 from: 32 Position 1 & 2 64 Position 3
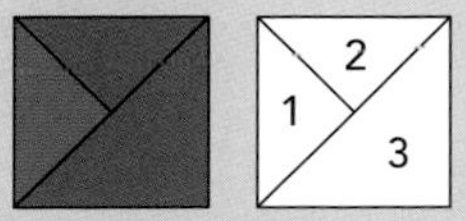 Block B	Make 12 from: 3 Position 1 & 2 6 Position 3	Make 16 from: 4 Position 1 & 2 8 Position 3	Make 18 from: 5 Position 1 & 2 9 Position 3 (yields 2 extra 1 & 2 units)
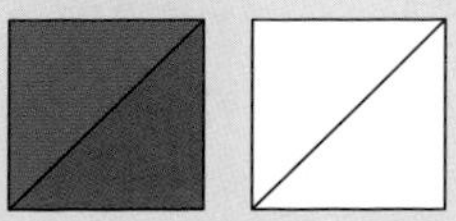 Block C	Make 4 from: 2 green 5" × 5" squares & 2 print 5" × 5" squares; trim to 4½" × 4½"	Make 4 from: 2 green 6" × 6" squares & 2 print 6" × 6" squares; trim to 5½" × 5½"	Make 4 from: 2 green 7" × 7" squares & 2 print 7" × 7" squares; trim to 6½" × 6½"

QUILT ASSEMBLY			
	46″ × 46″ Quilt	68″ × 68″ Quilt	86″ × 98″ Quilt
Quilt center layout	7 × 7 blocks 28½″ × 28½″	9 × 9 blocks 45½″ × 45½″	9 × 11 blocks 54½″ × 66½″

BORDERS AND BINDING Strips are cut across width of fabric, selvage to selvage.			
Fabric	46″ × 46″ Quilt	68″ × 68″ Quilt	86″ × 98″ Quilt
Green	• Join 7 strips 2″ wide; cut: 2 pieces 28½″ long (1st inner) 2 pieces 31½″ long 2 pieces 33½″ long (3rd inner) 2 pieces 36½″ long • Join 5 strips 1½″ wide; cut: 2 pieces 44½″ long (outer) 2 pieces 46½″ long	• Join 11 strips 2¼″ wide; cut: 2 pieces 45½″ long (1st inner) 2 pieces 49″ long 2 pieces 52″ long (3rd inner) 2 pieces 55½″ long • Join 7 strips 2″ wide; cut: 2 pieces 65½″ long (outer) 2 pieces 68½″ long	• Join 14 strips 2½″ wide; cut: 2 pieces 54½″ long (1st inner) 2 pieces 70½″ long 2 pieces 62½″ long (3rd inner) 2 pieces 78½″ long • Join 9 strips 4½″ wide; cut: 2 pieces 78½″ long (outer) 2 pieces 98½″ long
Pink	• From 4 strips 1½″ wide, cut: 2 pieces 31½″ long (2nd inner) 2 pieces 33½″ long	• Join 6 strips 2″ wide; cut: 2 pieces 49″ long (2nd inner) 2 pieces 52″ long	• Join 7 strips 2½″ wide; cut: 2 pieces 58½″ long (2nd inner) 2 pieces 74½″ long
Binding	• Cut 5 strips 2″ wide	• Cut 7 strips 2″ wide	• Cut 10 strips 2″ wide

BLOCK BORDERS			
	46″ × 46″ Quilt	68″ × 68″ Quilt	86″ × 98″ Quilt
Blocks per row	• Top and bottom, each: 9 A Blocks	• Top and bottom, each: 11 A Blocks	• Top and bottom, each: 11 A Blocks
	• Each side: 9 A Blocks plus 2 C Blocks	• Each side: 11 A Blocks plus 2 C Blocks	• Each side: 13 A Blocks plus 2 C Blocks

BLOCK CONSTRUCTION

This quilt is composed of 3 block types. The A Block is used for most of the quilt center and the outer pieced border, the B Block runs horizontally and vertically from the center square of plain fabric, and the C Block is used for the pieced border corners.

BLOCK C

The C Block is made with 2 half-square triangles. Place squares of green and print right sides together. Cut once diagonally from corner to corner. Stitch ¼″ from the bias edge. Press toward the print. Trim to the size indicated in the Block Construction chart. Make 4 blocks. These blocks are used in the pieced border corners.

Quilt Assembly

1. See the Quilt Assembly chart, diagram, and project photo to arrange the blocks, noting that each size quilt uses a different number of blocks. The largest quilt has one extra row at the top and bottom. Stitch the blocks together into rows. Press the rows in alternating directions.

2. Stitch the rows together to complete the quilt center. Press the seam allowances to one side.

Quilt assembly diagram, 68″ × 68″

Borders

1. Use the Borders and Binding chart to prepare the green 1st inner border strips.

2. Stitch the 2 short 1st inner border pieces to the top and bottom of the quilt and the 2 long pieces to the sides of the quilt. Press the seams toward the border.

3. Repeat Steps 1 and 2 for the pink 2nd inner border strips.

4. Repeat Steps 1 and 2 for the green 3rd inner border strips.

5. Stitch 4 rows of A Blocks together for the pieced ribbon borders using the Block Borders chart for the number of blocks and the Quilt Assembly diagram as a rotation guide. Make adjustments as necessary to the pieced border to ensure that it matches the size of the quilt center. Stitch the rows to the top and bottom of the quilt. Press the seams toward the quilt center.

6. To each remaining ribbon border row, add a C Block to each end, checking the diagram for the color placement. Stitch the rows to the sides of the quilt. Press the seams toward the quilt center.

7. Repeat Steps 1 and 2 for the final green outer border strips. Press toward the outer border.

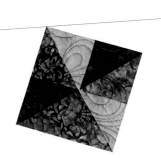

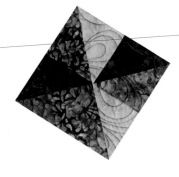

Pinwheel Puzzle

Pinwheel Puzzle is one of my favorite quilts. I love how everything interlocks and makes so many different pinwheels. Of all the quilts in this book, this one, to me, is the most surprising result of using only 1 block.

For this quilt, you have 3 size options: 55″ × 55″, 74″ × 74″, and 88″ × 88″.

FABRIC REQUIREMENTS Yardage is based on 42″-wide fabric unless noted.

Fabric	55″ × 55″ Quilt	74″ × 74″ Quilt	88″ × 88″ Quilt
Purple	1¼ yds	1⅝ yds	2¼ yds
Pink	1 yd	1⅜ yds	2 yds
Fuchsia	¾ yd	1⅛ yds	1⅝ yds
Green	½ yd	¾ yd	⅞ yd
Yellow	1⅝ yds	2⅝ yds	3½ yds
Purple (for binding)	½ yd	⅝ yd	⅔ yd
Batting	59″ × 59″	78″ × 78″	92″ × 92″
108″-wide backing	1⅔ yds	2¼ yds	2⅝ yds

CUTTING BLOCKS Strips are cut across width of fabric, selvage to selvage.

Fabric	55″ × 55″ Quilt	74″ × 74″ Quilt	88″ × 88″ Quilt
Purple	• From 2 strips 5½″ wide, cut: 9 squares 5½″ × 5½″ • From 5 strips 5″ wide, cut: 36 squares 5″ × 5″	• From 2 strips 6½″ wide, cut: 9 squares 6½″ × 6½″ • From 6 strips 6″ wide, cut: 36 squares 6″ × 6″	• From 2 strips 7½″ wide, cut: 9 squares 7½″ × 7½″ • From 8 strips 7″ wide, cut: 36 squares 7″ × 7″
Pink	• From 2 strips 5½″ wide, cut: 12 squares 5½″ × 5½″ • From 2 strips 5″ wide, cut: 16 squares 5″ × 5″	• From 2 strips 6½″ wide, cut: 12 squares 6½″ × 6½″ • From 3 strips 6″ wide, cut: 16 squares 6″ × 6″	• From 3 strips 7½″ wide, cut: 12 squares 7½″ × 7½″ • From 4 strips 7″ wide, cut: 16 squares 7″ × 7″
Fuchsia	• From 2 strips 5½″ wide, cut: 11 squares 5½″ × 5½″ • From 2 strips 5″ wide, cut: 16 squares 5″ × 5″	• From 2 strips 6½″ wide, cut: 11 squares 6½″ × 6½″ • From 3 strips 6″ wide, cut: 16 squares 6″ × 6″	• From 3 strips 7½″ wide, cut: 11 squares 7½″ × 7½″ • From 4 strips 7″ wide, cut: 16 squares 7″ × 7″
Green	• From 2 strips 5½″ wide, cut: 13 squares 5½″ × 5½″	• From 3 strips 6½″ wide, cut: 13 squares 6½″ × 6½″	• From 3 strips 7½″ wide, cut: 13 squares 7½″ × 7½″
Yellow	• From 4 strips 5½″ wide, cut: 25 squares 5½″ × 5½″ • From 1 strip 5″ wide, cut: 6 squares 5″ × 5″	• From 5 strips 6½″ wide, cut: 25 squares 6½″ × 6½″ • From 1 strip 6″ wide, cut: 6 squares 6″ × 6″	• From 5 strips 7½″ wide, cut: 25 squares 7½″ × 7½″ • From 2 strips 7″ wide, cut: 6 squares 7″ × 7″

BORDERS AND BINDING Strips are cut across width of fabric, selvage to selvage.

Fabric	55″ × 55″ Quilt	74″ × 74″ Quilt	88″ × 88″ Quilt
Yellow	• Join 11 strips 2″ wide; cut: 2 pieces 48½″ long (1st inner) 2 pieces 51½″ long 2 pieces 52½″ long (outer) 2 pieces 55½″ long	• Join 14 strips 3½″ wide; cut: 2 pieces 60½″ long (1st inner) 2 pieces 66½″ long 2 pieces 68½″ long (outer) 2 pieces 74½″ long	• Join 17 strips 4″ wide; cut: 2 pieces 72½″ long (1st inner) 2 pieces 79½″ long 2 pieces 81½″ long (outer) 2 pieces 88½″ long
Pink	• Join 6 strips 1″ wide; cut: 2 pieces 51½″ long (2nd inner) 2 pieces 52½″ long	• Join 7 strips 1½″ wide; cut: 2 pieces 66½″ long (2nd inner) 2 pieces 68½″ long	• Join 9 strips 1½″ wide; cut: 2 pieces 79½″ long (2nd inner) 2 pieces 81½″ long
Binding	• Cut 6 strips 2″ wide	• Cut 8 strips 2″ wide	• Cut 10 strips 2″ wide

BLOCK CONSTRUCTION Use Clip & Flip Pressing.

Sketch numbered blocks and glue small pieces of fabric to them to remind you of your color placement. Follow the directions for making Y Blocks on pages 5–9.

	55″ × 55″ Quilt	74″ × 74″ Quilt	88″ × 88″ Quilt
Finished block size	4″ × 4″	5″ × 5″	6″ × 6″
Position 1 & 2 square size	5½″ × 5½″	6½″ × 6½″	7½″ × 7½″
Position 3 square size	5″ × 5″	6″ × 6″	7″ × 7″
Block A	Make 36 from: 9 Position 1 & 2 18 Position 3	Make 36 from: 9 Position 1 & 2 18 Position 3	Make 36 from: 9 Position 1 & 2 18 Position 3
Block B	Make 16 from: 4 Position 1 & 2 8 Position 3	Make 16 from: 4 Position 1 & 2 8 Position 3	Make 16 from: 4 Position 1 & 2 8 Position 3
Block C	Make 8 from: 2 Position 1 & 2 4 Position 3	Make 8 from: 2 Position 1 & 2 4 Position 3	Make 8 from: 2 Position 1 & 2 4 Position 3
Block D	Make 24 from: 6 Position 1 & 2 12 Position 3	Make 24 from: 6 Position 1 & 2 12 Position 3	Make 24 from: 6 Position 1 & 2 12 Position 3
Block E	Make 16 from: 4 Position 1 & 2 8 Position 3	Make 16 from: 4 Position 1 & 2 8 Position 3	Make 16 from: 4 Position 1 & 2 8 Position 3
Block F	Make 28 from: 7 Position 1 & 2 14 Position 3	Make 28 from: 7 Position 1 & 2 14 Position 3	Make 28 from: 7 Position 1 & 2 14 Position 3
Block G	Make 12 from: 3 Position 1 & 2 6 Position 3	Make 12 from: 3 Position 1 & 2 6 Position 3	Make 12 from: 3 Position 1 & 2 6 Position 3
Block H	Make 4 from: 2 pink 5″ × 5″ squares & 2 yellow 5″ × 5″ squares; trim to 4½″ × 4½″	Make 4 from: 2 pink 6″ × 6″ squares & 2 yellow 6″ × 6″ squares; trim to 5½″ × 5½″	Make 4 from: 2 pink 7″ × 7″ squares & 2 yellow 7″ × 7″ squares; trim to 6½″ × 6½″

QUILT CENTER ASSEMBLY—ALL SIZES					
Row 1	Unit 1	Unit 3	Unit 1	Unit 3	Unit 1
Row 2	Unit 3	Unit 2	Unit 4	Unit 2	Unit 3
Row 3	Unit 1	Unit 4	Unit 1	Unit 4	Unit 1
Row 4	Unit 3	Unit 2	Unit 4	Unit 2	Unit 3
Row 5	Unit 1	Unit 3	Unit 1	Unit 3	Unit 1

BLOCK CONSTRUCTION

The A through E Blocks are used in the quilt center and the F, G, and H Blocks are used in the pieced border.

BLOCK H

The H Block is made with 2 half-square triangles. Place squares of pink and yellow fabric right sides together and cut once diagonally from corner to corner. Stitch ¼″ from the bias edge. Trim to the size given in the Block Construction chart. Use Clip & Flip Pressing by clipping the seam allowance and pressing counterclockwise from the back side. These blocks will be used in the pieced border corners.

QUILT ASSEMBLY

1. Arrange and sew the A through E Blocks into Units 1, 2, 3, and 4 as shown. Press toward the Position 3 fabric, clipping where necessary. The remaining Y Blocks will be used in the pieced border rows.

Unit 1—Make 9.

Unit 2—Make 4.

Unit 3—Make 8.

Unit 4—Make 4.

2. Lay out Units 1 through 4 using the Quilt Assembly chart, diagram, and project photo as guides to form the quilt center. Stitch the blocks together into rows and press the rows in alternating directions. Then stitch the rows together to form the quilt center.

Quilt assembly diagram

BORDERS

1. See the Quilt Assembly diagram to lay out the pieced border rows, using 7 F Blocks and 3 G Blocks for the top and bottom rows. For the side rows, again use 7 F Blocks and 3 G Blocks with 2 H Blocks. Be sure to double-check the placement of the G Blocks with the Quilt Assembly diagram because it can be a bit tricky.

2. Stitch the blocks into rows. Stitch the border rows to the top and bottom of the quilt, nesting the seams as you go. Press the blocks after you stitch, and press the long seam allowance to one side. Then add the side border rows to the quilt and press again.

3. Use the Borders and Binding chart to prepare the yellow inner border strips. You will cut the outside border strips later.

4. Stitch the 2 short inner border pieces to the top and bottom of the quilt and the 2 long pieces to the sides of the quilt. Press toward the outside.

5. Repeat Steps 3 and 4 to add the pink border strips and then the yellow outer border strips.

Trails of Illusion

This quilt has the look of a complex art quilt yet the simplicity of a One Block quilt. Actually, there are only 4 colorations of the block, and the only thing that changes is the Position 2 fabric!

For this quilt, you have 2 size options: 60″ × 70″ and 88″ × 100″.

FABRIC REQUIREMENTS Yardage is based on 42"-wide fabric unless noted.

Fabric	60" × 70" Quilt	88" × 100" Quilt
Dark green	$1\frac{3}{4}$ yds	$3\frac{1}{2}$ yds
Multi-dot	$2\frac{1}{8}$ yds	$3\frac{1}{2}$ yds
Yellow	$\frac{3}{8}$ yd	$\frac{1}{2}$ yd
Light green	$\frac{7}{8}$ yd	$1\frac{1}{2}$ yds
Aqua	$\frac{7}{8}$ yd	$1\frac{1}{4}$ yds
Medium green	$\frac{7}{8}$ yd	$1\frac{3}{8}$ yds
Dark green (for binding)	$\frac{1}{2}$ yd	$\frac{2}{3}$ yd
Batting	64" × 74"	92" × 104"
108"-wide backing	$1\frac{7}{8}$ yds	$2\frac{5}{8}$ yds

CUTTING BLOCKS Strips are cut across width of fabric, selvage to selvage.

Fabric	60" × 70" Quilt	88" × 100" Quilt
Dark green	• From 6 strips $6\frac{1}{2}$" wide, cut: 32 squares $6\frac{1}{2}$" × $6\frac{1}{2}$" 2 squares 6" × 6"	• From 8 strips $7\frac{1}{2}$" wide, cut: 38 squares $7\frac{1}{2}$" × $7\frac{1}{2}$" 2 squares 7" × 7"
Multi-dot	• From 11 strips 6" wide, cut: 64 squares 6" × 6"	• From 16 strips 7" wide, cut: 78 squares 7" × 7"
Yellow	• From 1 strip $6\frac{1}{2}$" wide, cut: 3 squares $6\frac{1}{2}$" × $6\frac{1}{2}$"	• From 1 strip $7\frac{1}{2}$" wide, cut: 3 squares $7\frac{1}{2}$" × $7\frac{1}{2}$"
Light green	• From 2 strips $6\frac{1}{2}$" wide, cut: 9 squares $6\frac{1}{2}$" × $6\frac{1}{2}$"	• From 3 strips $7\frac{1}{2}$" wide, cut: 11 squares $7\frac{1}{2}$" × $7\frac{1}{2}$"
Aqua	• From 2 strips $6\frac{1}{2}$" wide, cut: 9 squares $6\frac{1}{2}$" × $6\frac{1}{2}$"	• From 2 strips $7\frac{1}{2}$" wide, cut: 10 squares $7\frac{1}{2}$" × $7\frac{1}{2}$"
Medium green	• From 2 strips $6\frac{1}{2}$" wide, cut: 11 squares $6\frac{1}{2}$" × $6\frac{1}{2}$"	• From 3 strips $7\frac{1}{2}$" wide, cut: 14 squares $7\frac{1}{2}$" × $7\frac{1}{2}$"

BORDERS AND BINDING Strips are cut across width of fabric, selvage to selvage.

Fabric	60" × 70" Quilt	88" × 100" Quilt
Light green	• Join 5 strips $1\frac{1}{2}$" wide; cut: 2 pieces $40\frac{1}{2}$" long (1st inner) 2 pieces $52\frac{1}{2}$" long	• Join 7 strips $2\frac{1}{2}$" wide; cut: 2 pieces $54\frac{1}{2}$" long (1st inner) 2 pieces $70\frac{1}{2}$" long
Medium green	• Join 6 strips 2" wide; cut: 2 pieces $42\frac{1}{2}$" long (2nd inner) 2 pieces $55\frac{1}{2}$" long	• Join 7 strips $2\frac{1}{2}$" wide; cut: 2 pieces $58\frac{1}{2}$" long (2nd inner) 2 pieces $74\frac{1}{2}$" long
Aqua	• Join 6 strips $1\frac{1}{2}$" wide; cut: 2 pieces $45\frac{1}{2}$" long (3rd inner) 2 pieces $57\frac{1}{2}$" long	• Join 8 strips $2\frac{1}{2}$" wide; cut: 2 pieces $62\frac{1}{2}$" long (3rd inner) 2 pieces $78\frac{1}{2}$" long
Dark green	• Join 6 strips 2" wide; cut 2 pieces $47\frac{1}{2}$" long (4th inner) 2 pieces $60\frac{1}{2}$" long	• Join 8 strips $3\frac{1}{2}$" wide; cut: 2 pieces $66\frac{1}{2}$" long (4th inner) 2 pieces $84\frac{1}{2}$" long • Join 10 strips $2\frac{1}{2}$" wide; cut: 2 pieces $84\frac{1}{2}$" long (outer border) 2 pieces $100\frac{1}{2}$" long
Binding	• Cut 7 strips 2" wide	• Cut 10 strips 2" wide

BLOCK CONSTRUCTION Use Clip & Flip Pressing.

Sketch numbered blocks and glue small pieces of fabric to them to remind you of your color placement. Follow the directions for making Y Blocks on pages 5–9.

	60″ × 70″ Quilt	88″ × 100″ Quilt
Finished block size	5″ × 5″	6″ × 6″
Position 1 & 2 square size	6½″ × 6½″	7½″ × 7½″
Position 3 square size	6″ × 6″	7″ × 7″
Block A	Make 12 from: 3 Position 1 & 2 6 Position 3	Make 12 from: 3 Position 1 & 2 6 Position 3
Block B	Make 36 from: 9 Position 1 & 2 18 Position 3	Make 44 from: 11 Position 1 & 2 22 Position 3
Block C	Make 34 from: 9 Position 1 & 2 17 Position 3 (yields 1 extra 1 & 2 unit)	Make 40 from: 10 Position 1 & 2 20 Position 3
Block D	Make 42 from: 11 Position 1 & 2 21 Position 3 (yields 1 extra 1 & 2 unit)	Make 55 from: 14 Position 1 & 2 28 Position 3 (yields 1 extra 3 unit)
Block E	Make 4 from: 2 multi-dot 6″ × 6″ squares & 2 dark 6″ × 6″ squares; trim to 5½″ × 5½″	Make 4 from: 2 multi-dot 7″ × 7″ squares & 2 dark 7″ × 7″ squares; trim to 6½″ × 6½″

BLOCK CONSTRUCTION

Remember that the dark background fabric always goes in Position 1, so it will be on top when you make your first diagonal cuts. The multi-dot fabric is always in Position 3.

BLOCK E

The E Block is made with 2 half-square triangles. Place squares of dark green and multi-dot print right sides together. Cut once diagonally from corner to corner. Stitch ¼″ from the bias edge. Use Clip & Flip pressing by clipping the seam allowance in the center and pressing counterclockwise from the back. Trim the block to the size given in the Block Construction chart. Make 4 blocks. The E Block is used in the pieced border corners.

QUILT ASSEMBLY

1. Use the Quilt Assembly chart, diagram, and project photo as guides to lay out the blocks for the quilt center. The shaded areas in the chart represent the additional blocks required for the larger-sized quilt.

2. Stitch the blocks into rows, pressing the rows in alternating directions. Stitch the completed rows together to complete the quilt center.

QUILT ASSEMBLY Shaded area is for larger size quilt.									
Row 1	D	D	C	D	C	D	D	D	D
Row 2	D	C	B	B	B	C	B	D	B
Row 3	D	B	A	A	B	B	C	B	D
Row 4	B	A	A	A	A	B	C	C	C
Row 5	C	A	A	A	A	B	B	C	B
Row 6	C	B	A	A	B	B	B	C	B
Row 7	C	B	B	B	B	C	C	C	C
Row 8	B	C	B	B	C	C	C	D	C
Row 9	D	B	C	C	C	C	B	D	D
Row 10	D	D	B	B	C	B	D	D	B
Row 11	D	D	B	C	C	D	D	B	D

Quilt assembly diagram, 60″ × 70″

BORDERS

1. Stitch the light green 1st inner border strips together end-to-end diagonally to form one long strip. Cut the strip according to the Borders and Binding chart.

2. Stitch the 2 short 1st inner border pieces to the top and bottom of the quilt and the 2 long pieces to the sides of the quilt. Press toward the border.

3. Repeat Steps 1 and 2 for the medium green 2nd inner border, the aqua 3rd inner border, and the dark green 4th inner border.

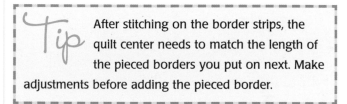

Tip After stitching on the border strips, the quilt center needs to match the length of the pieced borders you put on next. Make adjustments before adding the pieced border.

4. Make a pleasing arrangement with the remaining blocks for the pieced border rows, using the Quilt Assembly diagram and project photo as guides. The 60″ × 70″ quilt requires 10 blocks for the top and bottom and 12 blocks plus 2 half-square triangle (the E Block) blocks for each side. The 88″ × 100″ quilt requires 12 blocks for the top and bottom and 14 blocks plus 2 half-square triangle (the E Block) blocks for each side. Since the photo is of the smaller-sized quilt, arrange the remaining blocks any way you like for the larger-sized quilt or see *Flames Early Light*, page 58. Stitch the blocks into rows, press the seams to one side, and sew the rows to the top and bottom of the quilt and then to the sides. Press the seams toward the quilt center.

5. Repeat Steps 1 and 2 for the outer dark green border only for the larger quilt.

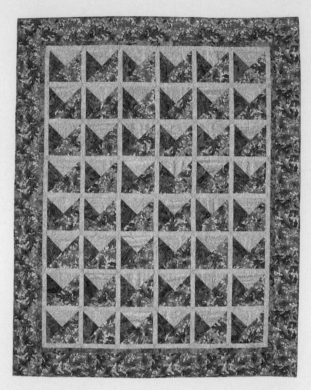

November, 61″ × 77″, 2005 Cheryl Malkowski.

Floral Triangles All Around, 71″ × 71″, 2005 Cheryl Malkowski.

 *Gallery*

One of the best parts of designing quilts is seeing what other people do with your ideas. Here are a few more of my quilts and some that my friends and students have made. Most are variations of patterns in this book, and all are patterns I designed. Of course, they're all made from just one block!

Sun Over a Pyramid Play, 62″ × 82″, 2006 Cheryl Malkowski. Pieced and quilted by Ramonda (aka. Charlie) V. Weckerle.

Flames Early Light, 88″ × 100″, 2006 Cheryl Malkowski. Pieced by Ruby L. Kosola. Quilted by Jane Yurk.

Harvest Star, 50″ × 67″,
2006 Cheryl Malkowski. Pieced by Judy Byrd.
Quilted by Jane Yurk.

Kite Tails, 30″ × 36″, 2006 Cheryl Malkowski.
Pieced and quilted by Julia Raynor.

Ribbons, 52″ × 72″, 2005 Cheryl Malkowski.

Aqua Trails, 63″ × 73″, 2006 Cheryl Malkowski.
Pieced and quilted by Jane Yurk.

Illusions, 60″ × 70″, 2006 Cheryl Malkowski.
Pieced by Teri Wells. Quilted by Lisa J. Taylor.

Columbus Day Storm, 52″ × 62″,
2006 Cheryl Malkowski. Pieced by Debbie Bennett.
Quilted by Beth Grubb.

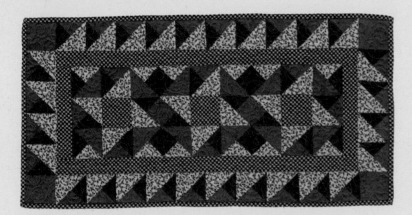

Twisty Star Table Runner, 36″ × 18″, 2006 Cheryl Malkowski.
Pieced by Sue Kelley. Quilted by Beth Grubb.

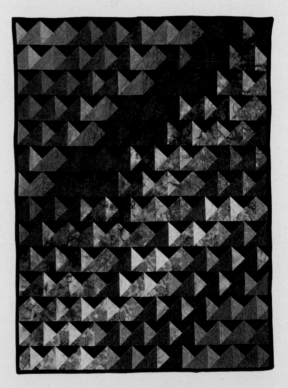

Pyramid Color Play, 50″ × 70″,
2006 Cheryl Malkowski. Pieced by Dolores Williams.
Quilted by Beth Grubb.

Jenny's Garden, 59″ × 59″, 2005 Cheryl Malkowski.

Triple Floral Whirlwind, 54½″ × 71″,
2005 Cheryl Malkowski. Pieced by Rosaley Smith.
Quilted by Cheryl Malkowski.

Floral Pinwheel Puzzle, 74″ × 74″,
2005 Cheryl Malkowski.

Kelsey's Windowpanes, 88″ × 88″, 2006 Cheryl Malkowski.
Pieced and quilted by Cheryl L. Meredith.

Giant Whirligig Wallhanging, 46″ × 46″,
2005 Cheryl Malkowski.

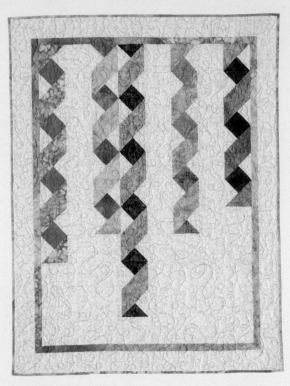

Baby Ribbons, 40″ × 52″, 2005 Cheryl Malkowski.

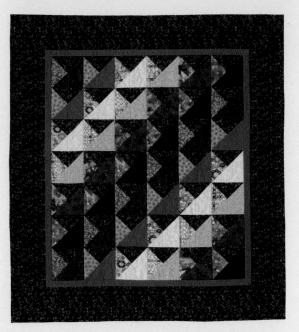

Pasha's First Quilt, 43″ × 48″,
2006 Cheryl Malkowski.
Pieced and quilted by Cheryl Seibel.

Baby Whirlwind, 50″ × 62″,
2005 Cheryl Malkowski.

Retro Twisty Star, 59″ × 72″,
2006 Cheryl Malkowski.

Resources

For a list of other fine books from C&T Publishing, ask for a free catalog:

C&T Publishing, Inc.
P.O. Box 1456
Lafayette, CA 94549
(800) 284-1114
Email: ctinfo@ctpub.com
Website: www.ctpub.com

For quilting supplies:

Cotton Patch Mail Order
3405 Hall Lane, Dept. CTB
Lafayette, CA 94549
(800) 835-4418
(925) 283-7883
Email: quiltusa@yahoo.com
Website: www.quiltusa.com

NOTE: Fabrics used in the quilts shown may not be currently available as fabric manufacturers keep most fabrics in print for only a short time.

C&T Publishing's professional photography services are now available to the public. Visit us at www.ctmediaservices.com

The 6½" square Omnigrip rulers, Omigrid Glow-Line Tape, and Collins Machine Seam Gauge and Adhesive Guide are all available from Prym Consumer USA. Ask for them at your local quilt shop.

PRYM CONSUMER USA
www.dritz.com
Phone: (800) 845-4948

Many of the quilts in this book were quilted with beautiful King Tut quilting thread by Superior Threads. Made from extra-long-staple Egyptian cotton, it is a pleasure to work with and candy for the eye. To check on availability in your area, go to www.superiorthreads.com and click on the store locator.

SUPERIOR THREADS
P.O. Box 1672
St. George, UT 84771
Phone: (435) 652-1867

Photo courtesy of Terry Day.

About the Author

Cheryl Malkowski lives in Roseburg, Oregon, with her husband, Tom, and their dog, Bosco. She feels her greatest achievements are her son and daughter, both of whom are successful young professionals. Cheryl has been quilting for fourteen years and publishing patterns for seven. Her first book, *Easy Chenille Appliqué: Create Dimension the Color Stick Way,* was released by C&T Publishing in January 2005. It presents a technique she developed that enables quilters to make quilts with the feel of an old chenille bedspread. She spends her time teaching, designing, doing longarm quilting, gardening, studying the Bible, playing music, and letting the dog in and out.

For information about Cheryl's pattern company (cheryl rose creations), workshops, lectures, and ways to contact her, visit **www.cherylmalkowski.com**.

Great Titles
from

C&T PUBLISHING